SO YOU WANT TO BE THE BOSS?

CAREER HIGHLIGHTS
of
J.W. (BILL) McLEAN

- 40 years in banking—26 as a chief executive officer;
- has held national leadership roles in credit, marketing, and management;
- architect of two major regional banking mergers, each becoming the leader in its respective market;
- one of three founding consultants of American Bankers Association's CEO School
- named Regional Banker of the Year for 1972;
- elected president of Federal Advisory Council of the Federal Reserve System in 1979;
- authored, edited, or contributed to:
  - *Fundamental Principles of Sound Bank Credit . . . Say Yes or Say Why*
  - *Cross-Selling Bank Services to Business*
  - *Loan Officers Handbook*
  - *Commercial Banking Handbook*
- his "Let's Talk Business" campaign won the George Washington Honor Medal Award of the Freedom Foundation;
- holds highest honorary degrees from two universities;
- early exponent of "Leadership through INWARD MARKETING";
- Adjunct Professor of Business Administration and Chairman of Business Administration Board of Advisors, University of Oklahoma;
- Past President and current Chairman, Oklahoma Heritage Association.

SO YOU WANT TO BE THE BOSS?

A CEO's Lessons in Leadership

J. W. McLean

Prentice Hall, Englewood Cliffs, New Jersey 07632

Library of Congress Cataloging-in-Publication Data

McLean, J. W.
    So you want to be the boss? a CEO's lessons in leadership / J.W. McLean.
        p.   cm.
    Includes bibliographical references.
    ISBN 0-13-815432-5
    1. Leadership. 2. Chief executive officers. 3. Executive ability.   I. Title.
    HD57.7.M397 1990
    658.4'09--dc20   89-28370
                                                                    CIP

Editorial/production supervision
  and interior design: Elaine Lynch
Cover design: Lundgren Graphics, Ltd.
Manufacturing buyer: Ray Sintel

 © 1990 by Prentice-Hall, Inc.
A division of Simon & Schuster
Englewood Cliffs, New Jersey 07632

The publisher offers discounts on this book when ordered in bulk quantities. For more information, write:

> Special Sales/College Marketing
> Prentice-Hall, Inc.
> College Technical and Reference Division
> Englewood Cliffs, NJ 07632

All rights reserved. No part of this book may be
reproduced, in any form or by any means,
without permission in writing from the publisher.

Printed in the United States of America

10 9 8 7 6 5 4 3 2 1

ISBN 0-13-815432-5

PRENTICE-HALL INTERNATIONAL (UK) LIMITED, *London*
PRENTICE-HALL OF AUSTRALIA PTY. LIMITED, *Sydney*
PRENTICE-HALL CANADA INC., *Toronto*
PRENTICE-HALL HISPANOAMERICANA, S.A., *Mexico*
PRENTICE-HALL OF INDIA PRIVATE LIMITED, *New Delhi*
PRENTICE-HALL OF JAPAN, INC., *Tokyo*
SIMON & SCHUSTER ASIA PTE. LTD., *Singapore*
EDITORA PRENTICE-HALL DO BRASIL, LTDA., *Rio de Janeiro*

THIS BOOK IS
DEDICATED TO
THE READER

WHO

GROWS

A

LITTLE

TALLER

AS

HE OR SHE

READS

IT.

CONTENTS

SO YOU WANT TO BE THE BOSS?

Hopefully your answer is "YES," but only if you understand all that this means in terms of the basic knowledge required and the necessity of making a basic commitment to *seek, acquire,* and *apply* that knowledge, as follows:

PREFACE   xi

1   UNDERSTANDING OF SELF   1

To learn precisely what your own natural tendencies are and how you can best use, improve, or compensate for them.

A Long Renowned Aphorism 1, But an Acorn Can Become Only an Oak Tree 2, The Versatility Scale 4, An Expert Is a Guy Who Has Made All His Mistakes in One Field 4, The Prima Donna Tendency 6, Versatility—for Individual Growth 8, The Masks of a Loser 9, So, What's Your Basic Seed—or Need? 10

2   UNDERSTANDING MANAGEMENT STYLES   13

To learn about the conventional styles of CEO decision making, the characteristics of each, and an array of their common mistakes.

Today, Tomorrow, and Yesterday 13, As Simple as XYZ 13, But Beware of Management by "Bull Session" 15, The Acid

Pitfalls to Be Avoided   116,   The "Clean Exit"—A Skill or an Art?   117,   Brains: The Ultimate Asset   118

10   UNDERSTANDING CEO STRESS   121

To learn the indispensable value both to the organization and self of physical, mental, and emotional care and pacing.

A Very Bad Joke   121,   The Other Extreme   121,   Our Objective   122,   Stress Levels   122,   Finding an Elusive Remedy   124,   Lose a Job—Gain a Career   130,   The Mood Meter   131,   Are Gurus Now Out?   131,   Remember Your Roots   134,   Stress: Not Yet an "Endangered Species"   135

11   BONUS CHAPTER: UNDERSTANDING WHY BOSSES FAIL   137

To learn some of the more common forms of failure and oft repeated mistakes to be avoided at the top.

A Quick Disclaimer   137,   Why Chapter 11?   137,   On Being a Secure Winner   138,   The Don'ts Revisited   139,   The MPM Revisited   139,   My Favorite 15 Failures   140,   Poor Personnel Selection: A Root Cause   151,   Procrastination: A Still Deadly Sin   151,   organize, Organize, ORGANIZE   152,   The Dreaded Risk of Failure Kills Time   152,   Failing Really Isn't All Bad   153

EPILOGUE   155

The costly trade-offs involved in serving as a chief executive in return for its unique rewards.

INDEX   163

PREFACE

The dual purpose of *So You Want to Be the Boss?* is (a) to *identify* and (b) to *enhance awareness* of the essential ingredients involved in functioning effectively as a *chief executive*. What inspired it requires a candid and somewhat personal disclosure.

But for the consistent support and timely assistance—more accurately, the pushes and shoves—of others, this may well have become one of those countless millions of books only dreamed, never written. The dream itself began in the fall of 1958 when at age 36 I was recruited by Houston's then fourth-largest bank. Its chairman, an outside director, informed me that I "*might* become its chief executive in three to five years" (it actually happened in less than a year). He next said something that became emblazoned on my psyche: "I *hope* you'll be ready." His emphasis on the words "might" and "hope" lay heavily on my conscience from that moment on because I knew better than anyone that my readiness was hardly born, much less mature.

It was this acknowledged inadequacy that pushed me to read and study (and experiment with) everything I could find on the subject of CEO preparation, competence, and performance, a subject on which I had been collecting material passively for about a decade. The search seemed endless, yet rewarding, and over time I felt my efforts were yielding some remarkably useful guideposts. But until this day I have not found a complete chronicle on this enormous subject, one that begins where I hungered for guidance in those early years and ends where I still needed it at age 65, my normal retirement age, in the spring of 1987.

Therefore, for your consideration, whether remarkable or

this job; perhaps I could have filled in some of my missing skills in a much more orderly fashion than I subsequently decided to do so."[1]

Knowledge, therefore, of one's own *natural tendencies* and how best to use, improve, or compensate for them is clearly the premier criterion for successfully being the boss. How fortunate it is that others who share this concept have already developed reliable approaches not only for knowing ourselves better but also for recognizing key characteristics in others.

BUT AN ACORN CAN BECOME ONLY AN OAK TREE

Yes, the natural tendency of an acorn—properly nurtured—is to grow into a stately oak, not an elm, maple, or hickory. But you did not need to read this to confirm that earthshattering discovery. Its corollaries, however, may well be worth consideration, especially since they form the basic thesis for this entire work:

- *Nobody is born with all of the ready-made characteristics of a successful chief executive officer, the "stately oak" of the business world.*
- *Such characteristics are skills that can be learned, rather than talents that either are or are not endowed at birth.*
- *It is also possible to detect at a fairly early age an individual's tendencies with respect to his or her "task" versus "people" orientation and relative "assertiveness."*

The founder of Wilson Learning Company (a premier motivational/growth counseling group), Larry Wilson, sums up the latter concept in an enlightening grid (figure 1). By analysis of the response to a hundred confidential personality questions from five good friends (not family members), Wilson claims that he can readily plot one's position on the grid within one of its four quadrants:

1. (upper right) the *assertive task-oriented type*—THE DRIVER

---

[1] Richard D. Harrison, chairman and CEO, Fleming Companies, Inc., Oklahoma City, letter to the author, 20 December 1988.

But an Acorn Can Become Only an Oak Tree

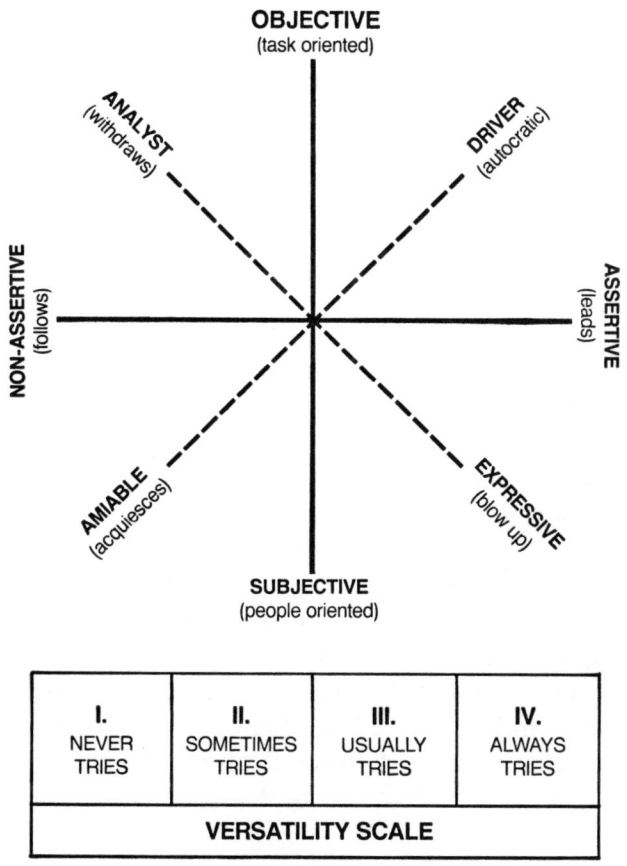

Figure 1

2. (lower right) *the assertive people-oriented type*
   —THE EXPRESSIVE
3. (lower left) the *nonassertive people-oriented type*
   —THE AMIABLE
4. (upper left) the *nonassertive task-oriented type*—
   —THE ANALYST.

He next describes a reliable method of confirming the accuracy of such a simplistic classification of people according to these four basic types involving what he calls their *backup systems,* that is, how they behave when challenged or thwarted. It goes like this:

The DRIVER becomes *autocratic.*
The EXPRESSIVE *blows up.*
The AMIABLE *acquiesces.*
The ANALYST *withdraws.*

In other words, since you rarely have the opportunity to interrogate five close friends of each individual you need to know well, a reasonably reliable alternative is available. *Notice how they behave under stress* and take advantage of that telltale knowledge—their *backup system*—to position them on the personality grid and, in turn, gain invaluable insight on how to predict and deal with them.

THE VERSATILITY SCALE

Unlike the acorn, *some* (but by no means *all*) of us have the capacity to modify our behavior and consciously substitute tendencies befitting a given situation. The "versatility scale" below the "personality grid" (figure 1) presents four stages of proficiency in terms of at least making the effort. How effective or not the results may be when one endeavors to become more versatile, the scale itself is an invitation to risk trying it in return for the occasional triumph.

AN EXPERT IS A GUY WHO HAS MADE ALL HIS MISTAKES IN ONE FIELD

More importantly, what a valuable tool for a potential chief executive to be able to assess his or her own tendencies and decide which of the four broad grid categories fits best. Such knowledge, moreover, can also be invaluable in becoming more versatile in dealing with others.

1. The effective CEO becomes more or less assertive, depending on the job dynamics and personalities involved.

An Expert Is a Guy Who Has Made All His Mistakes in One Field

2. The effective CEO senses when to become focused more on the task or the people, again, as dictated by the job dynamics and personalities involved.

It is, of course, essential to realize that there are no preferred locations on the grid; no quadrant is superior or inferior to any other. Indeed, many brilliant successes in business have been those who have known very well what their natural tendencies were and either used, improved, or compensated for them in their quest for greater *versatility*.

Joseph Conrad said, "To be a great autocrat, you must be a great barbarian" (*Forbes,* July 27, 1987).

Henry Miller said, "Whatever needs to be maintained through force is doomed" (*Forbes,* July 27, 1987).

Perceptive DRIVERS have learned to be less assertive on occasions when reverting to the autocrat would only delay—or perhaps prevent—a solution altogether. Enlightened ANALYSTS have found that a more expressive dialogue can sometimes do wonders toward a solution when withdrawal would only prolong, if not defeat, further progress entirely. However difficult it may be for EXPRESSIVES to resist a "blowup" when things seem completely hopeless, the mature ones know that a more composed and patient analytical attitude can occasionally open up an entirely new and productive approach. Similarly, many well-adjusted AMIABLES have learned how important it can be at times for them to be more assertive in pursuit of the task rather than remain preoccupied with seeking the approval of others involved in the process.

Like the "guy who made all his mistakes in the same field" and ultimately became recognized as an "expert," DRIVERS, EXPRESSIVES, AMIABLES, and ANALYSTS can persist stubbornly along their respective paths of greatest tendency and sometimes do reasonably well. However, those who learn to know themselves well enough to realize who they really are, where they are clearly deficient, and how to become genuinely more versatile in dealing with others will soon find that their levels of effectiveness can be enhanced enormously.

Who cares if he never makes "expert"? They will be too preoccupied with new challenges, new skills, and—sure—a few defeats, but constantly presented with exciting new opportunities far beyond their former reach.

THE PRIMA DONNA TENDENCY

Seeking refuge in one's "backup system" can be a costly choice, while resisting the urge can pay significant dividends. Although none of the following examples (one for each quadrant) leaped out at me at the time as a lesson in self-knowledge, in hindsight they certainly seem worthy of careful note today.

Case 1. One of the most AMIABLE people I have ever known worked patiently with me in my earliest days in banking, when several others and I were trying to learn the rudiments of double-entry posting in the promissory note window. He really knew the subject, and he taught it thoroughly. But I guess Clarence (not his real name) was just too nice, if you know what I mean. Nothing offensive—he was just a thoroughly nice guy. When something went wrong, whether he was responsible or not, he was always saying, "I'm sorry, I'm sorry."

You could sense that his supervisor enjoyed Clarence's subservience. As a matter of fact, it was almost as though Clarence himself would have been delighted to spend his entire career in the note window. And, sure enough, he nearly did. It was only after more than five years of training a couple of dozen of us that Roger (not his real name either) and I practically demanded that Clarence be given a chance for something better. It worked, but for another seven precious years of his career—although I didn't think of it in those terms then—this consummate AMIABLE continued to revert to his natural tendency to *acquiesce* when tested or challenged.

But one day (I think as a result of his devoted wife's insistence) Clarence finally *asserted* himself. He actually threatened to resign and—amazingly—did it without having another job lined up. While that is not often a recommended strategy, it was so out of character for Clarence that it really got management's attention. They were so shocked they pro[moted] him immediately. He had finally resisted his *backup* [system an]d had become a more *versatile* individual. In his new [role] he was the epitome of self-confidence, having learned [to assert] himself when necessary, and he was well on his way

The Prima Donna Tendency

to becoming one of the bank's top business development officers.

Case 2. Looking back, I quickly recall two classic cases of the ANALYST type, each of whose painstaking attention to detail won the admiration of their superiors during their early years but who experienced enormous discomfort later when finally elevated to the CEO level. In fact, in each case it simply did not take. But in the case of Harold (not his real name) there is already a happy ending. Seemingly he finally decided to risk a more *subjective* demeanor when things became sticky, rather than merely to *withdraw* and let others grapple with the problem. Learning how disastrous that can be for a chief executive, Harold simply became more *versatile*. He now has landed another top job in another city, and the reports of his early success as a more people-oriented executive are gratifying indeed.

Case 3. The best example of a DRIVER type who learned the hard way how becoming *autocratic* when tested can be much too costly—is me. It occurred in my second year as a CEO. I will never forget it. At the first Discount Committee Meeting of the new year, I couldn't wait to do it! You see, for months in advance I had made a note every time one of the loan officers had indicated he would "take care of it *right after the first of the year.*" So the first item of business on January 3, 1960, was to start around the table looking each member straight in the eye and ask questions such as, "Bob, here are the four major things you have told me you would handle 'right after the first of the year.' Let's review them right now because today the new year is already three days old, etc., etc." And so it went, awkwardly, around the table, one after another, because each had procrastinated in the same way.

Yes, it's true that they had all put things off, but I did not have to make the point by humiliating each one in the presence of the others. What an *autocratic* thing to do. Why, oh why, couldn't I have done it one-on-one. I suppose I didn't think I had the time. But believe me, I spent much more time trying to repair my relationships over the months ahead, and to this day I know that I am a lot slower to play the *autocrat* when a hurdle seems unreasonably high.

Case 4. When *EXPRESSIVES* revert to their *backup system,* everyone knows it, and my memory is filled with examples. In fact, the *blowups* I have witnessed when otherwise exceedingly competent people yielded to frustration are all too sadly indelible in my mind. One of the reasons I recall them so well is that I have since come to realize that those very *blowups* themselves actually accounted for the fact that the victims *never really achieved their full potential afterwards.* What a shame that such a manageable personality trait literally ruins so many careers. Yet what board of directors could ever entrust the CEO reins of a viable business to an executive who, no matter how effective when things go well, is subject to temper tantrums just when a cool head is needed most.

But quite fortunately, not all expressives need be condemned to such a fate. The answer, again, is to be found in learning—no, *determining*—to be more *versatile,* indeed, somehow to realize that there will be times when one must rein in those wonderful emotions that usually make the expressive far superior to the three other basic types in the all important *subjective* skills. No one thought that Dave (not his real name) could change his ways, and frankly neither did I. But after his heart attack, either by choice or necessity he pulled it off. Here was a genuinely effective producer of profitable new business. But now and then administrative details gave him fits, and he would take it out on whoever was nearby. I'm sure he knew it had held him back as steadier though less productive juniors passed him by. But he closed his career at normal retirement much more *versatile* professionally and much more at peace with himself and everyone around him personally.

VERSATILITY—FOR INDIVIDUAL GROWTH

In the four cases just cited, the individual—each representative of a different quadrant on the Personality Grid—was able to grow professionally by becoming more *versatile* (see lower portion of figure 1 for the "versatility scale"):

Case 1—The AMIABLE became more assertive and led in business development.

Case 2—The ANALYST became more people-oriented, less withdrawn, and is succeeding in a top job in another city.

Case 3—The DRIVER learned to resist his autocratic tendency and focus more upon the personal needs of others.

Case 4—The EXPRESSIVE found that his outbursts only prevented him from achieving his full professional potential.

This is not to say that any one of these four classic examples has yet reached stage "IV. ALWAYS TRIES" on the versatility scale. Even attainment of stage "II. SOMETIMES TRIES" can do wonders in most of our lives. For many of us, a much tougher objective will be stage "III. USUALLY TRIES." But, in any case, individual growth—whether professional or personal—begins with the recognition of *versatility* as the necessary catalyst. This at least will move one past debilitating stage "I. NEVER TRIES."

THE MASKS OF A LOSER

No one walks around with the label "LOSER" on his or her lapel. Yet just as surely as you can usually place someone on the personality grid, there are several almost infallible signs—let's call them masks—that often can identify the individual who never quite makes it.

MASK 1: THE SKIPPER. Perhaps the easiest to spot is the hail fellow who greets you with a winning smile, but who at age 40 is now in his ninth or tenth job. He has skipped from one to the next so often that his average tenure is barely a year with almost as much time out of work as his time employed. How he has maintained employment is beyond all comprehension. But on he goes, skipping through an aimless career, always making sure he leaves before he loses.

MASK 2: THE SUBTLE CYNIC. These are tougher to know immediately. She takes delight in showing up contemporaries or giving them "faint praise." They are always out to trip someone up but without appearing to have done so deliberately. What a shame that such otherwise talented people become so entangled with the game of trying to win at the expense of others—and only succeed in being inevitably unmasked for the losers they really are.

MASK 3: THE HYPERACTIVE. Some losers of this persuasion go undetected for years. They are not drifters nor are they devious. They are constantly in motion and seem far more preoccupied with activity than purpose. They seem to possess limitless energy and never, ever finish anything. Their incredible addiction to misdirected effort is often mistaken by superiors for creativity, and they can hide behind their unconscious loser's mask indefinitely.

MASK 4: THE ULTRACONSERVER. Finally we have perhaps the most insecure of all employed losers—and the one who may never be found out. Every business, of course, requires an expense custodian or comptroller to monitor budget compliance and prevent waste. But lurking in the middle ranks of many successful businesses is the individual—usually a veteran employee—who takes great delight in killing promising projects in their early stages before there is any revenue to justify support.

The damage these losers do is incalculable. Sure, they always appear to be saving significant sums by terminating new projects in their embryo stages, and senior management is hard pressed to go along in consideration of bottom-line pressures—as opposed to what is best in terms of *maximum sustainable long-range earning power* (much more about this later).

SO, WHAT'S YOUR BASIC SEED—OR NEED?

If you are still in doubt as to what your own basic tendencies are with respect to "tasks" versus "people," the ground-breaking studies of David C. McClelland may be useful. In the early 1950s he concluded that in our culture, at least, there are two distinct inner characteristics that drive many of us much of the time: (a) the *need for achievement* and (b) the *need for power*. While there are, of course, other needs, one of these two is usually dominant, especially in *assertive* people and may even transcend intelligence as a key to successful performance.

So, What's Your Basic Seed—or Need?

Those driven by the former (n-Achievement) tend to set tough goals; they enjoy taking personal responsibility and risking new ventures. In short, they are *more objective than subjective*. Those driven by the latter (n-Power) are quite different in that they are much more concerned with the impact they have on others through persuasion and control. In short, they are *more subjective than objective*.

Please do not think that you are odd if you can recall circumstances that found you in both camps. Perhaps you have already gained subconscious *versatility*. But few of us are really that psychologically ambidextrous. Thus you should really be able to focus on your dominant tendency and decide which orientation truly best describes the basic you, that is, *what makes you tick*. When you have done so, you will have gained enormous and invaluable insight for your future effectiveness inasmuch as the great majority of us are completely unaware of such things.

Through it all, however, it will be well to recall regularly the reassuring words of the renowned Presbyterian clergyman, Dr. William M. Elliott, Jr., in a sermon he delivered more than 40 years ago to his Highland Park congregation: "Like David, who on that notable day determined to be himself, the greatest gift any man can offer to the world is *just himself—at his best*. Each of us is a bit of God's unrepeated handiwork, and we only handicap our usefulness when we attempt to assume some unintended role."

Once having embraced this wonderfully enabling outlook, you will also be best prepared to consider and possibly employ, as needed, one or more of the *basic management styles* presented for your consideration in the next chapter.

Chapter 2

UNDERSTANDING MANAGEMENT STYLES

It's better to be ready and not go, than to go and not be ready.
—Anonymous

TODAY, TOMORROW, AND YESTERDAY

This subject could easily consume all our remaining pages. Instead, however, this chapter's purpose is simply to present the *conventional* ways in which successful executives manage daily decisions, how they approach tomorrow's decisions, the author's observations concerning each, some key "don'ts" from yesterday, and, finally a (do-it-yourself) executive report card.

AS SIMPLE AS XYZ

In terms of how the chief executive orchestrates the daily decision-making process, writers of management literature generally concur in identifying three basic styles:

Theory X—in which the *leader makes* all the important decisions[1]

Theory Y—in which lower-level *employees participate* in the decision-making process[2]

Theory Z—in which decisions are made by *consensus*[3]

Recent data, compiled by the Albers School of Business at Seattle University from a comprehensive survey of chief executive officers, shows that Theory Y is the popular choice of the vast majority of the nation's top corporate leaders. Clearly, the participative aspects of Y also achieve *partial responsibility* of the group for results, an all-important ingredient clearly missing from autocratic Theory X. This is something the enlightened CEO knows all too well and sometimes makes the case for Theory Z consensus decision making, which transfers *full responsibility* to the group.

Wilson Learning Company diagrams this concept quite effectively with a slightly different nomenclature:

TELL—means the executive "tells" the group the important decisions (as in Theory X).

SELL—means the executive and the group participate in decision making almost equally (as in Theory Y).

JELL—means the executive lets the decision "jell" through consensus by the group (as in Theory Z).

Following this approach, as you will observe in figure 2, the *responsibility* for the results varies directly with the degree to which the *authority* is shared between the executive and the group.

---

[1] Douglas McGregor, *The Human Side of Enterprise* (New York: McGraw-Hill Book Co., 1960), pp. 33–34.

[2] Ibid.

[3] Lyndall F. Urwick, "*Theory Z,*" *S.A.M. Advanced Management Journal*, vol. 35 (January 1970), pp. 14–21.

THE DECISION DIAGONAL

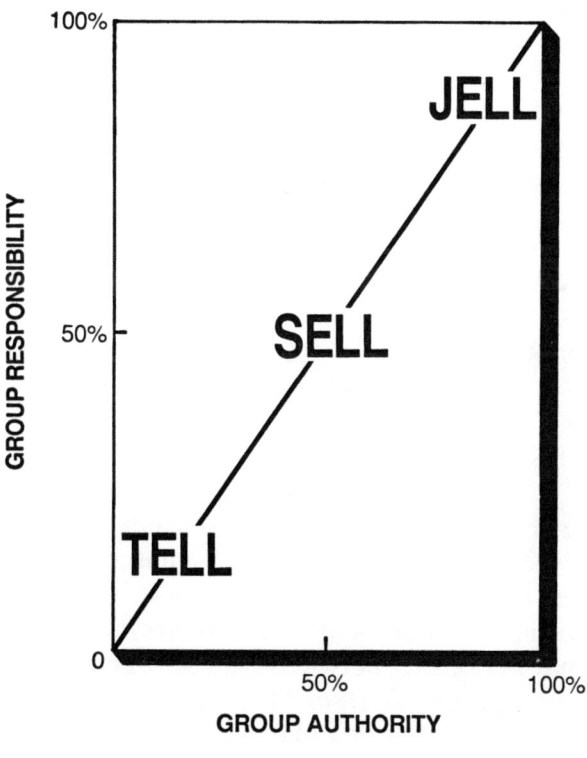

Figure 2

BUT BEWARE OF MANAGEMENT BY "BULL SESSION"

As desirable as it is to have large *group responsibility* for the results of *key* decisions, experienced CEOs also know very well that, when Theory Z becomes the predominant methodology, members of the group come to expect that all (or nearly all) decisions will be resolved in that same manner. Key decision making is heady stuff, and *consensus* decision making can consume excessive time that often prevents other key decisions from receiving unhurried consideration. Even worse, the temptation within the group for loquacious debate—the dreaded "bull session"—is both an expensive trade-off and a not very healthy or reliable precedent to establish.

Two suggestions seem in order for those executives who nevertheless would prefer to risk a reasonable number of Theory Z decisions:

1. Hold the *size* of the group to a manageable number.
2. Provide the chosen members of the group with a *written* digest of the key issues well in advance.

In this way, a much more channeled participation can be achieved, while the executive is perceived to be much less the authoritarian creature he might otherwise appear to be under Theory X, in which he decrees, or Theory Y, in which he persuades.

THE ACID TEST

Also, having chosen "Y" or "Z," the seasoned executive will not be dismayed by the *interpersonal sparks* that may fly among those asked to make decisions. When *sparks* are flying, you are about to get the best from everyone—*no short circuits please!* Of course, the real criterion for choosing between X, Y, or Z is: *can the executive afford to gamble on the outcome?* Once he has opted for Y or Z, he must let the process unfold, and he must be bound by the outcome. Option X is lost forever on that particular decision.

This is precisely why the author has become convinced that, more and more, *the ultimate effectiveness of the CEO over the tenure of the office may well be the extent to which she is consistently able to delineate between those decisions that can safely be entrusted to the participative or consensus process from those that only she should decide.*

AS SIMPLE AS MBO

The prolific Peter Ferdinand Drucker, author of 22 books, is the acknowledged inventor in 1954 of "management by objective" (MBO),[4] a widely used management technique for sorting out and

---

[4] Peter F. Drucker, *The Practice of Management* (New York: Harper & Row, 1954), p. 8.

tackling *future business decisions*. But for all his erudition, practitioners of MBO seem to veer off in countless directions, and the finished product too often is only a mutation of the parental model. The acronym MBO has been described as "*a process whereby the superior and subordinate managers of an organization jointly identify common goals, define individual areas of responsibility in terms of the results expected for use in measuring and assessing performance.*"[5]

The sequence of steps[6] sometimes used is as follows:

1. An individual submits written performance objectives for the coming year, with specific plans and target dates for observing them.
2. The individual and his boss discuss and either agree upon or modify the objectives and the plan.
3. The individual and his boss periodically review the plan and make revisions, as needed.
4. At year-end, a self-appraisal of performance and results is discussed with the boss.
5. A new set of objectives is established for the next year.

NOT SO FAST, PETER

In this writer's view, however, the above process—while far superior to those that begin with planning rather than goal setting or implementation ahead of planning—is flawed for not having begun with the indispensable first step: RESEARCH. In fact, there are at least three forms of research that demand consideration preliminary to goal setting. In the order of their magnitude, they are:

1. *Economic*. Goals and plans can hardly be viable without an early assessment of both "macro-" and "micro-" economic considerations.

---

[5] George Odiorne, *Management by Objective: A System of Managerial Leadership* (New York: Pitman Publishing, 1965), p. 55.

[6] Henry Migliore, *MBO: Blue Collar to Top Executive* (Washington, D.C.: The Bureau of National Affairs, Inc.), p. 22.

2. *Market.* Similarly, realistic goals must relate to competitive factors, as well as each market's demographic elements.
3. *Organizational.* Research within the organization itself can be tremendously revealing in pointing up serious voids in the staff's table of organization that must be addressed prior to embarking upon otherwise unrealistic—if not unattainable—efforts.

If all this seems elementary, do not be surprised by the dozens of examples across corporate America in which arbitrary goal setting and planning take place virtually "in a vacuum" with little or no regard for questions such as:

- Will the economy remain stable long enough for our goals to be reached?
- Are our goals too ambitious in consideration of our main competitor's already commanding lead in our most lucrative markets?
- Has the goal-setting process made a genuine assessment of the human resources and operational support required for success?

CONSIDER THIS MASTER PLANNING MODEL (MPM)

While we would not presume to reinvent "Drucker's wheel," perhaps we can sum it all up, at least in outline form, in a master planning model (MPM)[7] in FIVE KEY STEPS:

Step 1—RESEARCH
- economic (conditions/trends)?
- market (needs/competition)?
- organizational (strengths/weaknesses)?
- other (political, sociological, etc.)?

---

[7] The MPM format was developed over time by the author with staff input beginning in 1965, while he was serving as Director of Marketing for Bank of America, San Francisco.

Step 2—GOAL SETTING
- urgent (now)
  short-term (12 months)
- medium-term (2 to 4 years)
- long-term (5 plus years)

Step 3—PLANNING
- crisis plan
- profit plan
- intermediate plan
- master plan

Step 4—IMPLEMENTATION
- who?
- what?
- when?
- how?

Step 5—MONITORING RESULTS
- the "scorecard"
- incentive compensation
- mid-course correction
- research for new goals

In other words, while goal setting and planning can make the difference between an organization on the move and one that drifts, neither can be more than a superficial exercise without the companion steps of research, implementation, and monitoring results. In Chapter 5, we will see how useful—indeed essential—this five-step approach can be to the development of superior earning power.

CRISIS MANAGEMENT

It would insult the reader's intelligence for the author to suggest all business crises can be solved in the same basic way. Any such claim, of course, would be preposterous. There is, however, a very useful *methodology-template* that can often be employed advantageously. Its principal virtue is its "divide and conquer" approach because the common nature of many crises is the growth of their rapid-fire challenges, which often multiply at a cancerous rate.

The method involves three basic steps:

STEP 1: *Quickly distinguish between the problem and the symptoms* (the ratio can be as high as ten symptoms for each real problem).

STEP 2: *Quickly determine who is most affected by the problem and who needs to be involved in the solution* (usually not everyone need be involved).

STEP 3: *Deliberately develop alternatives for eliminating the crisis* (it sometimes gets pretty simple, if it can be dealt with at all).

The action words are *distinguish, determine,* and *develop.* You have now done your *research.* And next, of course, you are ready to set your *goals,* adopt your *plans, implement* them, and *monitor* results.

You may want to consider using this quick template in your next crisis when there is insufficient time to do a more comprehensive and prolonged analysis.

The *Wall Street Journal* of (January 8, 1988), featured a story on the worst inland oil spill in our history—the one that plagued Ashland Oil and its chief executive, John R. Hall. The *Journal* stated that "Mr. Hall decided against devoting a three-hour Monday morning meeting solely to the spill. He believed the crisis was being handled well and didn't demand all of his attention. He was wrong."

Would our methodology-template have saved the day?

Who can say.

At least, stripping away the *symptoms* (STEP 1) would have revealed the public relations nightmare as the real *problem* after everything possible was already being done to contain the disaster physically. At least, devoting more attention to the *who* needed to be involved in the solution (STEP 2) just might have resulted in more of the senior staff being thoroughly immersed in the details for which the media were clamoring and perhaps have avoided some of the troublesome discrepancies that later occurred in the news.

DO AS I SAY, NOT AS I DID

So much for the *theories of management style* in dealing with the pressing decisions. But what *practical lessons* can be learned from CEO mistakes of yesterday? Here our data abound. For whatever the world thinks of chief executives as a group, they are their own worst critics—and that is at least refreshing!

Next for your consideration, then, is a tabulation of DON'Ts that some CEOs have admittedly learned too late. An unsuccessful effort was made to group them logically, but this was abandoned in behalf of spontaneity (even at the expense of some redundancy, but hopefully no contradictions):

- DON'T establish control at the expense of stifling initiative.
- DON'T be insensitive, aloof, abrasive, arrogant, or intimidating to anyone—whatever his or her station.
- DON'T betray a trust.
- DON'T fall into a narcissistic style (or even a perceived one) by seeking the praise and recognition of others.
- DON'T interrupt.
- DON'T contribute needlessly to the paper blizzard.
- DON'T create false deadlines.
- DON'T procrastinate.
- DON'T stifle communications.
- DON'T make unrealistic promises.
- DON'T be insecure.
- DON'T waste time worrying about things beyond your control.
- DON'T mask insecurity with a workaholic lifestyle.
- DON'T mask insecurity with an alcoholic lifestyle.
- DON'T put off the toughest task until last.
- DON'T let meetings drift.
- DON'T even meet until you know what the meeting should accomplish.
- DON'T fail to make decisions as you read the mail.

- DON'T fail to delegate.
- DON'T fail to follow up.
- DON'T delegate your obligation to long-term planning.
- DON'T expect hasty verbal direction to be carried out precisely, if at all.
- DON'T ever stop looking for ideas.
- DON'T hesitate to discard ideas when it is clear they are not likely to be productive.
- DON'T be an easy prey to ego-feeding civic activities.
- DON'T fail to pay your civic rent.
- DON'T let difficult people change your course.
- DON'T let unexpected setbacks change your course.
- DON'T let anything change your course when you know it's right.
- DON'T become a victim of organizational incest.
- DON'T engage outside talent purely for the sake of diversity.
- DON'T be satisfied with traditional pay policies.
- DON'T shake them up until you know it's fair to do so.
- DON'T become a victim of ravenous personal involvement when it's something you like, or overdelegation when it's something you don't like.
- DON'T ask more of others than you ask of yourself.
- DON'T fail to leave time for the unexpected, which usually happens once a day.
- DON'T neglect family.
- DON'T neglect self.
- DON'T neglect your creator, and finally
- DON'T *expect to comply with even one of these consistently without making a regular, conscious commitment to it.*

DO THE TOUGHEST THINGS FIRST

So much for the FORTY DON'Ts.

How many times have you put off doing something difficult or unpleasant that you knew perfectly well you were going to have to do eventually? One of the most prevalent forms of this debilitating habit is the seductive tendency to request an extension beyond April 15 for filing the Federal Income Tax Return. Internal Revenue Service officials have estimated that more than half of such requests should and easily could have been avoided.

The principal problem with this sort of procrastination is that the offender finally becomes so guilt-ridden about it that she becomes distracted and unable to deal efficiently with other matters. Interestingly, on the other side of it, if we fill each day only doing that which we enjoy, psychologists say it usually does not take long before we no longer enjoy what we do.

The inescapable conclusion for each of us, therefore, is to give much more priority to those tasks—even one task—that we have been putting off because we just did not feel like doing it. Why not deliberately give it a try tomorrow morning? No one should feel too worldly or sophisticated to do so. You just might be surprised at the result in terms of how much better you will like yourself.

ARE YOU FLUNKING CEO?
A SELF-APPRAISAL EXAM

In January 1985, *Industry Week* reported on the creative work of James Clawson, associate professor of business administration at the University of Virginia, in the form of a self-test for conscientious CEOs (and executives who aspire to the top)* to determine whether they have the necessary ingredients in seven key areas. Here's *IW*'s adaptation of that test.

Even though some of the questions deal with subject matter we will consider later, GO AHEAD, BE BRAVE, find out if you're already "flunking" CEO. Or perhaps you will learn that, as a prospective boss, your instincts are all positive. In any case, if your inquiry into this subject is serious, *you do need to know*. Indeed, as you must know by now, that is the underlying theme of this entire book. Give yourself a score of 5 for each question answered "always," a 3 for each "sometimes," and a 0 if you answer "never."

* Used with permission of Professor James Clawson, Ph.D., Darden School, University of Virginia, Charlottesville, Virginia.

	A	S	N
1. When planning your company's financial policies, do you consider the impact over a ten-year period?	—	—	—
2. When making decisions, do you consider their implications for the community, the nation, and the world?	—	—	—
3. Are you honest with your fellowmen? In other words, do you "practice what you preach"?	—	—	—
4. How frequently do you ask yourself what your job or industry would be like if the "rules" were changed—perhaps by an unforeseen development or a technological breakthrough?	—	—	—
5. Do you ever write out your vision of the future of your company?	—	—	—
6. Do you plan the development of your company's talent for each key position?	—	—	—
7. Do you put department or divisional goals aside in order to achieve the company's overall objectives?	—	—	—
TOTAL SCORE	—	—	—

HOW DID YOU DO?

    30–35: You're a fine chief executive officer. Keep it up!
    24–29: You're not in serious trouble, but be prepared for some tough questions at the next board meeting.
    15–23: Better work on your weaknesses. The board may be getting restless.
    0–14: Have you updated your resume lately?

Here's hoping you had the courage to grade yourself without favor, because that is exactly the way your directors will do it.

THE MOST DREADED TEST: SUBORDINATE APPRAISAL

Some executives I have known were far more intimidated by employees than by directors or shareholders. The *fear of bad morale*, in some cases, was more dreaded than a "down" earnings report for an interim quarter. Lower earnings can be raised, but lowered morale is usually a *chronic problem* that can linger for years. Indeed, with some employees, a once-branded noncaring management can never reoccupy an esteemed status again.

Knowledge of this fact—the difficulty of regaining lost morale—has also given rise to the "let's rate the boss" phenomenon. In some cases it is merely an effort on the part of paranoid managers to let employees "blow off a little steam," while the enlightened ones recognize the trend as a genuinely direct way to learn how their management styles are perceived by juniors so that necessary changes can be made in order to do a better job at the top.

Whatever the motivation may be, the process now has a beachhead at a few alert places of business—even if most executives are still too reticent to stick their necks out. Of course, no one tries to measure his or her own worth precisely in micrometers, and admittedly the terms used are still quite general. In every case, I'm sure, top management is relieved when the dreaded test is finally over—but only until the next time.

Although factual findings on the process are limited, there is a growing sentiment that subordinates as a group are a more valid source of data concerning a manager's effectiveness than a single senior supervisor. Further, the use of *subordinate appraisals* is an ideal way in which to enhance perceptions of "employee participation" policies within the organization. The author's research of the ways in which this intriguing and relatively new device is being implemented yielded a wide variety of rating formats. The shortest and most general consisted of only five areas of inquiry, while another asks for ratings in twenty-two categories.

Professor Henry Mintzberg at McGill University in Montreal has developed a model of ten criteria that seems well suited for all-around use.[8] It calls for both subordinate and supervisory appraisal of a CEO as a(n):

- leader
- information disseminator
- crisis handler
- entrepreneur
- resource allocator
- environmental monitor
- liaison
- negotiator
- spokesman
- organizational representative

Professor Mintzberg then suggests six *graduated performance rankings* for each quality, that is, the subordinate or supervisor would *rank* the manager on a scale of 0 to 5, with respect to each criterion:

- not at all—0
- to a very limited extent—1
- to a limited extent—2
- to a moderate extent—3
- to a fairly large extent—4
- to a great extent—5

Of course, the "most dreaded test" has its detractors. Major concerns include (a) the fear that managers will focus on just trying to please subordinates; (b) the authority of the manager will be undermined; (c) subordinates are not qualified to rate managerial performance; (d) some seasoned managers will not stand for subor-

---

[8] Henry Mintzberg, *The Nature of Managerial Work,* cited in an article entitled: "How Would Subordinates Rate You?" (Best of Business Quarterly, Spring 1987), p. 81.

dinate appraisals and quit their jobs; (e) some subordinates may deliberately downgrade the manager if they have been in any way abused in the past; and (f) others will be paranoid about telling the truth.

Only the passage of more time will adjudicate the ongoing utility of *subordinate appraisals*. Meanwhile, it is the author's view that, at the very least, the approach automatically provides "feedback" to managers that they might not otherwise receive; if their "skins" are not too "thin," the process could yield early warnings of faulty managerial leadership.

MANAGEMENT OBSOLESCENCE

Can last year's successful management technique be next year's failure? Is the state of the art really changing that rapidly? Or do the basic principles of good management remain reliable year after year?

While generalizations on this subject are treacherous, it is the author's view, based on his own managerial trip, that the truth rests somewhere in between, that is, there really is an ongoing need to reassess constantly both the *role* and *function* of the enlightened manager, but without necessarily casting off tried and proven approaches.

Robert M. Randolph of Tulsa said it so clearly back in 1975 in his book *Planagement* (which won wide acclaim among members of the American Management Association), that we repeat here verbatim his treatise on *"the obsolete manager."*

> Who is the obsolete manager? What are his characteristics? Are there many obsolete managers in American industry? What makes the manager obsolete, and how can he reestablish himself as an effective producer? These are the questions most frequently asked when the problem of obsolete manager is discussed.
>
> The subject of personal obsolescence is a touchy one. Many good people teeter precariously on the ragged edge of complacency and are satisfied to manage momentum rather than potential. In order not to rock the boat, the manager riding the downside of his own

demise adopts the motto: My job is not to run the train/Or even clang the bell/But watch the train as it jumps the tracks/And see who catches hell.

Touchy or not, the problem of the obsolete manager must be objectively faced, compassionately understood, and empathetically dealt with. If organizations do not have this strength, then they will become custodians of their own demise.

Who is the obsolete manager? He is the manager who was born in 1920, died in 1965, and won't be buried until 1980. He is no longer growing and perceives challenge as a threat rather than an opportunity. He doesn't like himself, hates his job, is convinced there is a vast conspiracy dedicated to making waves in his sea of complacency. While he might agree that 80 percent of today's management practices are obsolete, he is content to leave the problem to those "young bucks" who will take over when he retires. What are some of his characteristics?

1. His predictions of the future are based only on past experiences, and he manages momentum, not potential. He has run out of challenges and is frustrated because he has not been able to establish new and self-actualizing objectives.

2. He concentrates on weaknesses rather than strengths—he knows what's wrong, not what's right—and this negative attitude makes him a pessimist who sees the difficulty in every opportunity rather than the opportunity in every difficulty. He is also defensive and unable to identify a direction for himself that would improve his unhappy situation.

3. This manager makes the simple seem complex, attempts to make himself indispensable, and won't delegate authority to others.

4. He judges people by their traits and actions rather than by the results they obtain. He is inclined to emphasize know-who much more than know-how.

5. He relies on numbers and data rather than on people. Since he doesn't believe in people (usually he thinks the behavioral sciences are a lot of "academic nonsense"), he is more of an exploiter than a builder. He trusts no one and considers personal survival the most important law.

6. This type of manager is a poor communicator and thus is constantly misunderstood. He is an anxious talker and a poor listener.

7. Mr. Obsolete is afraid of enthusiasm and extensively uses sarcasm or cynicism to dampen it. He takes credit but rarely gives it, and he is usually against an idea that was "not invented here."

Management Obsolescence

8. The basic strategy of this inept individual is to get. He prides himself on getting the best deal, rather than a fair deal. He knows more answers than questions, and he depends on the right to hire and fire for his authority rather than on earned privilege.

9. He manipulates people and prides himself on being an excellent politician. The other guy is the competition who may be after his job, so it becomes a business game to "get him first."

10. He frequently procrastinates rather than makes a decision he will be held responsible for.

11. The obsolete manager is more conscious of position and activity than of direction and results. The how is emphasized, not the why.

12. Frequently his approach is to establish a budget first, and then develop the plan the budget is supposed to support. Functional thinking is more pronounced than profit thinking.

13. He resists change, new ideas, and orderly procedures, and tends to avoid establishing proper policies, procedures, and paperwork.

14. The obsolete manager is pragmatic, dictatorial, and inflexible. He dislikes the participative management approach and is extremely protective of his prerogatives. To him, it is more important to establish his point than to find the truth or the best answer. He manages by his objectives and all others are subordinate.

15. This type of manager will not lead by example; his philosophy is "Do as I say, not as I do." He is disorganized, escapist, and undisciplined. He has no physical fitness program and rarely feels better than adequate. He lacks direction and priorities, and his judgments depend almost entirely on past experience, intuition, and emotion rather than on a balance between these important elements and a logical and factual approach.

Are there many obsolete managers in American industry? Unhappily, the answer is yes. When members of groups composed of managers, industrial psychologists, management educators, writers, consultants, and people engaged in management recruitment were requested to independently write down their estimate of how many United States managers in their thirties, forties, and fifties are obsolete, the answers were within 5 percent of each other. The number of obsolete managers in their thirties was established as 45 to over 50 percent; in their forties, 55 to 60 percent; and in their fifties, over 60 percent. Perhaps this is the same phenomenon observed by Dr. Peter when he stated in his now famous Peter Principle that everybody is destined to rise to his own level of incompetence.

The greatest danger to private enterprise may be that we have created a situation that produces a high number of obsolete managers who go home and tell their children how horrible their job and company are. Consequently, their children passionately reject the so-called establishment, and our hope for future improvement in the situation is in serious jeopardy.[9]

Author Randolph and I also happen to concur that what makes managers obsolete—or not—lies basically in the individual and his or her dedication to the ever-changing always-demanding task. But is it not so in other professions? The professional shoeshine person must be aware of and enhance his relative attractiveness in the marketplace or, you know what, the shoeshine machine will replace him. Indeed, in every occupation—certainly at the top—one must practice his skills regularly, if obsolescence is to be avoided.

Perhaps epic pianist Paderewski said it best: "If I miss one day of practice, I can tell it in my playing. If I miss two days in succession, my critics can tell it. If I miss a week, my audience can tell."

COMMITMENT AND INITIATIVE

Yes, a disciplined *commitment* to self-improvement is the *first key* antidote for the poison of management obsolescence. Fortunately, however, effective long-term managers need not be self-taught. Literally hundreds of seminars, conferences, videocassettes, audio tapes, and an accelerating stream of really credible books and monographs are available on command.

There is a powerful *second key* required for the conscientious manager to avoid becoming obsolete. It is a very plain thing called *initiative*.

The two keys, of course, are interrelated. One without the other will yield only sporadic results. I can recall many instances in my own struggle to manage when only one of the keys was present and nothing happened. One in particular may be worth sharing.

For months in the early 1970s I had reasoned that the speed of my reading—then about 550 words per minute when I made a total

[9] Robert M. Randolph, *Planagement* (New York: AMACOM, 1975), pp. 6–8.

Commitment and Initiative

effort—was not nearly what it should be if I was to free myself from the drudgery of daily reports, printouts, minutes, legal opinions, audits, memoranda, and correspondence, not to mention the regular periodicals, subscriptions, and financial news I really wanted to read. My 550-rate was not considered slow in those days, but I had heard about one hour per day self-learning courses that claimed to boost such speeds to the 1,000- to 2,000-word-per-minute level in only six weeks time. This sounded great to me—a way perhaps to triple my reading rate in only 42 hours. What dividends it would pay. Just think of the free time I would have!

We were scheduled to leave for a two-week Colorado vacation in about a month, so I exercised my initiative, bought the course, and thought to myself, "Why not spend 6 hours every other day in Colorado working on this thing, and get in the 42 hours that way rather than stretch it out over so many weeks? That would still leave 18 hours of each workday free and the odd days would be all clear for a well-earned vacation." What a sensational and productive way to get through August!

What happened was predictable, I suppose. The second day in the mountains I really did make the effort. In fact, I rigged up the entire apparatus—a springlike gadget that could be adjusted to variable speeds that would flash word combinations for quick recognition. It was fascinating. I could also see how it really would enhance one's reading skill. But two hours into the exercise I decided to take a break, and that did it. In another hour I was being picked up by an old friend who called and proposed a 9-hole warm-up before our scheduled 18-hole match the next day.

I don't think I touched the reading apparatus more than twice again the rest of the time for one "good reason" or another. It was as Winston Churchill once said, "There are usually two reasons for everything—an acceptable reason and the real reason."[10] My acceptable reason for not sticking with the plan that second day in the mountains was "not to reject an old friend." The real reason, of course, was that I really didn't want to spend my vacation that way.

I had demonstrated my *initiative* by sending for the course—the *second key* to self-improvement—but I had neglected to make a disciplined *commitment* to it—the essential *first key*. The two keys

---

[10] Winston S. Churchill, British prime minister, from a broadcast to Allied troops in World War II, via the *Armed Forces Radio Network* (December 1944).

must go in tandem for best results. Otherwise it is just too easy for *initiative* to give way to *complacency* and for *commitment* to bow to *procrastination.* The inevitable results:

> YOU ARE NOT NECESSARILY A BAD MANAGER
> —YOU'RE JUST OBSOLETE.

In any case, whatever style of management decision making appeals to you in any given situation, an elusive quality called *leadership* transcends them all. What it is, how it differs from *management,* and how to achieve it will be the subject of the next chapter.

Chapter 3

UNDERSTANDING LEADERSHIP

Better to follow than to lead uncomfortably.
—Anonymous

IN SEARCH OF LEADERSHIP

Some attempts to define leadership flounder from the sheer weight of their own compulsion to say everything possible about it. Still others contend that the versatile term defies an all-purpose definition altogether. The legendary Harold Geneen of ITT says, "It is purely subjective, difficult to define and virtually impossible to measure objectively."[1]

My own view is that Webster handled it fairly well: "*lead-er-ship n 1: capacity to lead; 2: ability to mold individuals into a team in pursuit of common objective.*"[2] The only objectionable word is "mold," for reasons that will be quite evident later. But if Web-

---

[1] *Managing* (New York: Doubleday, 1984), p. 127.
[2] *Webster's New Collegiate Dictionary* (Springfield, Mass.: G. & C. Merriam Co., 1979), p. 648.

ster's definition will serve for the moment as an acceptable raw definition, each of us is now free to fashion our own version, based, of course, on individual experiences and perceptions. Here are a few such twists for your consideration (some original, others borrowed, and some from long lost sources, but now virtually in the public domain):

- Leaders are just ordinary people with extraordinary determination.
- A leader's true value can usually be discerned by taking a close look at those doing the following.
- A leader is a person not to lean on, but one who makes leaning unnecessary.[3]
- A true leader accepts more than his or her share of the blame and less than his or her share of the credit.[4]
- The mantle of leadership is a subtle—even elusive—thing which more often than not is conferred upon the individual, rather than declared by the would-be leader; and
- Leadership is totally intangible—but the one thing we know is that we know it when we see it, usually in the form of elevated morale.[5]

Retired banker/economist Louis F. Danforth defines it succinctly in still another way: "There is a relatively simple definition of a successful leader. *First,* he knows where he wants to go; *second,* he knows how to get there; and, *third,* he is capable of either forcing or persuading enough of the people who count to go along with him." Danforth then adds, "This fits all the great leaders of history, both good and bad including: Julius Caesar, Washington, Lincoln, Lenin and Adolph Hitler."

Whether this truly defines leadership or perhaps only "transactional leadership" is a question we shall address later in this chapter.

[3] Danny Cox, Danny Cox Conventions & Seminars, Atlanta.
[4] Ibid.
[5] Walter Wriston, Chairman and CEO (retired), Citicorp, New York

A PERSONAL (IF NOT SCIENTIFIC) OBSERVATION

Returning to my own view once again—although I confess I have no formal research to document it—there definitely seems to me to be a *seductively magnetic force* that motivated the leaders I have known over the past 40 years. Frankly, I felt its unmistakable tug many times myself. It was not the status, not the power, not the recognition, and not even the prospect of large material gain that primarily inspired it. No! I am convinced that—in case after case—it was just *the chance to make a difference* that outweighed all other considerations combined. After all, who among us is immune to the irresistable pull of an historic achievement that will forever bear one's name—indeed, the *chance to make a difference!*

Further, whatever one's station in life may be, each of us has done his or her share of following. He who leads usually knows from prior personal experience how it feels to follow enthusiastically as distinguished from what it is like to be pushed. The key word is *feels*. Indeed, it has been the author's observation over the years that people follow others essentially because it *feels good* to do so. This, in fact, suggests the most basic of all definitions of leadership. If, in essence, it is all a matter of generating *good feelings* on the part of followers, we are now talking about a thing called *morale*.

So what better omnibus definition of leadership than "*the ability to enhance the morale of the follower.*" Anything less, it seems to me, is not true leadership.

WHAT LEADERSHIP IS NOT

There is a catchy little definition of leadership floating around which, in the author's view, is pitifully wide of the mark: "*the ability to inflict pain and get away with it.*" The notion that a good leader should be out to "inflict pain" is an unfortunate and highly negative concept. Indeed, if unchecked, it could turn out to be quite misleading—even dangerous.

To be sure, an effective leader sometimes must make tough decisions that require a disciplined adherence by others to a stern course. But she does so in quest of a rewarding objective from which all will benefit significantly. In this sense, those who follow need never feel pain, but rather a gratifying sense of determination and team achievement.

LEADERSHIP VERSUS MANAGEMENT

Whatever it is, however it occurs, the relationship of leadership to management is essential for an aspiring chief executive to understand. The now-renowned authors of *A Passion for Excellence* actually suggest that the words "managing" and "management" should be discarded in favor of "leadership"; that *management* connotes "controlling," "arranging," "demeaning," and "restricting," while *leadership* suggests "freeing," "building," "unleashing," "enabling," and—most importantly—"growing."[6]

Obviously not every professor of management on today's college campus would cheer for such a shocking notion. Indeed, a strong faculty contingent would hold that leadership is but *one alternative style* of management, and that good management embodies not only leadership but also an array of other techniques and skills.

It is not the author's purpose here to spark such a debate or even to inflame the one that Peters and Austin ignited. Rather, why bog down in such semantics when the real issue is simply to insure that those who are in charge will inspire a *maximum productive effort* from every other individual involved—call it whatever you will.

Another pair of prolific writers on this subject, in their book *Leaders,* put it this way, "Managers do *things right*, while leaders do the *right things*."[7] James A. Ogilvy wrote in the June 1987 edition of *Marketing Communications,* "The style of management inherited from the industrial era is incompatible with *information intensive businesses*. When the goal is *innovation* rather than *standardization*, a company needs *leaders* rather than *managers*."[8] Next, he quotes Pulitzer Prize-winning historian James McGregor

---

[6] Tom Peters and Nancy Austin, *A Passion for Excellence* (New York: Harper & Row, 1982), p. xvii.

[7] Warren Bennis and Burt Nanus, *Leaders*. (New York: Harper & Row, 1982), p. 21.

[8] Ogilvy is director of the Esaleu Institute Program (sponsored by the Ford Foundation) and a former professor of philosophy at Yale University.

Leadership versus Management

Burns, who has advanced the concept that "There are *two kinds* of leadership—one that sounds very much like *traditional management* and the other that comes much closer to the kind of leadership needed in the *information age*."[9] He calls the *first*, or managerial style, "*transactional*"; that is, "You give me 40 hours of hard work; I'll give you a paycheck." The *second* and more relevant style is called "*transformative*"; that is, endeavors to appeal to the followers rather than working against, or stifling, them.

Ogilvy further opines, "*Transformative leadership* isn't always easy, and the skills required aren't necessarily those taught in business school. We know how to *teach management;* but it's *not* at all clear that we know how to *educate leaders*. . . . Where can a company find leaders if the business schools can only train managers?" Obviously such an assertion tends to imply that no college campus is attuned to this "new enlightenment" and that all management curricula are somehow fatally flawed.

Not so.

Indeed, already on some campuses the term "entrepreneurship" is a prominent shibboleth augmenting "management." Of course, little is yet known as to the shape and form of the supporting resources or scope of instruction. But the basic intent, we are told, is to embody "leadership" principles and techniques. Meanwhile, Boone Pickens may have nailed the core difference between management and leadership in his latest book, when he said, "Leadership is taking risks and building confidence in yourself."[10] Let's think about that. How simple, and how completely it accounts for these oft-spoken gems:

> "A manager inspires subordinates to have confidence in him, while a leader inspires them to risk having confidence in themselves."[11] Indeed, the leader *risks* "inspiring" them in order to build team confidence.
>
> "A manager endeavors to make right decisions while a leader sometimes makes questionable decisions and then makes them right."[12] Indeed, the leader *risks* "making questionable deci-

---

[9] James McGregor Burns emeritus professor of political science, Williams College.

[10] *Boone* (Boston: Houghton Mifflin Company, 1987), p. 274.

[11] Charles "Tremendous" Jones, motivational consultant, Dallas.

[12] Ibid.

sions" because he believes there is a good chance of "making them right."

In the words of Dr. Willis J. Wheat, "Virtually every forward step in our society has been the reward of calculated risks taken by leaders who have spurned society for progress."[13]

CAN MANAGERS BECOME LEADERS

Writing in the *Harvard Business Review,* David Finn said, "No one knows today any more than Thomas Carlyle did in the nineteenth century *what makes a leader a leader.* . . . All I can add to his insight is that no one can be a leader if he or she doesn't permit his or her *deepest instincts as a human being* to manifest themselves. . . ."[14]

Frankly, when I stumbled onto this one, I almost gave up writing this book. How does one unleash "his or her deepest instincts" with any assurance of the outcome? Especially when some of our deepest instincts border on the psychotic!

A little later—quite by chance—I read in Harold Geneen's best seller, "The first obligation of any chief executive is to *set the goals* for his company . . . , *point his people in the direction of the goal posts* and tell them how to get there."[15] How can this be? (I thought). Here is one of the nation's most successful all-time industrialists who "SET ALL THE GOALS" . . . even "POINTED HIS PEOPLE" . . . and "TOLD THEM HOW TO GET THERE." What was he—coercive driver, domineering monarch, despotic tyrant, or just a darn good manager who did not elect to *risk* even the partial participation of his subordinates?

We shall never know. But we can wonder what the results might have been had the legendary Geneen used a more *participative* style, and how much more successful successor management

---

[13] Dean of business administration, Oklahoma City University, Oklahoma City.

[14] *Harvard Business Review,* Vol. 58, no. 6, p. 110.

[15] *Managing,* (Garden City, N.Y.: Doubleday & Company, Inc., 1989), p. 130.

might have been when he retired. What we do know is that, when he finally gave up the CEO mantle at ITT, the repercussions in terms of declining revenues (six consecutive down years) and net income (four out of six down years) were quite disappointing to shareholders.

In the words of James J. Cribben "To get employees to do mediocre work, one need only *drive them*. . . . To elicit their top performance, one must get them to *drive themselves;* and this requires a skill that relatively few executives master."[16] Yes, it is rare, but I firmly believe that managers can become leaders and it need not be only a relative few who make the transition successfully. Moreover, those who do will experience the incredible gratification that only comes from witnessing their own contribution to a common cause multiplied many times over when they have dared to empower others to "drive themselves."

If that sounds as if this chapter is advocating that next Monday morning all good managers who would suddenly become leaders should abandon decision-making Theories X and Y[17] and let everything be determined by consensus (Theory Z), then please read a little farther.

Instead, as suggested in the previous chapter, it is simply a matter of becoming more consistently able to delineate between those decisions that can safely be entrusted to the participative process from those which only the CEO must make. But how is the CEO to know unless he demands of himself more and more risk taking commensurate with the record of performance by the group?

ALTERNATIVE LEADERSHIP STYLES

Just as there are three generally accepted management styles (X, Y, and Z), there are at least four alternative leadership styles (A, B, C, and D) that can be useful in assessing the risk of group decision making, depending on the difficulty of the task and the experience of the group. Here is how they might look:

[16] *Effective Managerial Leadership,* (New York: American Management Association, Inc., p. 140.
[17] See Chapter 2, p. 14.

Style A—tough goal/inexperienced group—**DIRECTING**
- requires leader's *high task* orientation
- requires leader's *high people* orientation

Style B—tough goal/experienced group—**COACHING**
- requires leader's *high task* orientation
- does not require leader's *high people* orientation

Style C—easy goal/inexperienced group—**ENABLING**
- does not require leader's *high task* orientation
- requires leader's *high people* orientation

Style D—easy goal/experienced group—**DELEGATING**
- does not require leader's *high task* orientation
- does not require leader's *high people* orientation[18]

As I have reflected on the *symmetry* of these basic styles of leadership, I have come to realize that they are neither formidable nor mysterious after all. Indeed, if I ever succumb to writing another book, I already have the title: *Leaders Don't Do Magic.* Instead, I suspect the best ones think a lot about the degree of difficulty of the *task,* the *experience* of the *group,* and then move confidently ahead with *their own appropriate orientation—* no "sleight of hand" involved at all! As a long successful CEO, Jack Durland, once put it, "The secret of success is not magic—it only seems like it. People who think it is magic will never achieve it."[19]

LEADERSHIP'S ULTIMATE REWARD

Admittedly the term leadership has multiple meanings and interpretations. It is a versatile concept with an almost endless variety of applications. But it is distinctly different from management in that it dares to *enable* and encourages *creativity* in others, as distinguished from controlling and commanding. While a skillful leader will retain both authority and responsibility when the task is too severe for the

[18] Adapted (but only in part) from Paul Hersey and Kenneth H. Blanchard, *Management of Organizational Behavior, 3d ed.* (Englewood Cliffs, N.J.: Prentice Hall, 1977), pp. 103–04.

[19] Durland served as president and CEO of Cains Coffee Company, Inc., Oklahoma City, 1950–1981.

subordinates' level of competence, an enlightened leader constantly strives for more and more participation by the group.

Leadership then—in its highest form—becomes, in itself, a process of *successful risk-taking* (more "wins" than "losses") and definitely a few *lessons in fatigue* from trying to "make questionable decisions right."

A fair question at this point: "What will cause a CEO to feel best about himself as he reflects on all those unrecoverable years?"

From my own 40-year experience, 26 of which were spent as a CEO, I have no hestitancy in saying the ultimate reward of leadership is to be able to say at the end of the day, "I saw someone grow again today, and *I helped*."

And finally, the SUMMA-ultimate reward is when one of those "someones growing" is *oneself*.

If stimulating individual growth is the key to leadership, Chapter 4 on "Understanding Motivation" and how to "get the best out of others" is the next logical extension of our inquiry.

Chapter 4

UNDERSTANDING MOTIVATION

How to lose friends and antagonize people.
—Anonymous

EXPECT FRAILTY IN OTHERS

One of Will Rogers' lesser-known but most perceptive sayings was, "Even if you're on the right track, you'll get run over if you just sit there." Could he have had in mind one of the greatest obstacles confronting the leader who attempts to motivate others: COMPLACENCY?

In her widely syndicated column, Erma Bombeck talks about "all those people who spend the productive years of their lives sitting around whining that there's nothing to do."[1] A more positive corollary might well be that "*success comes to those who wait but only if they work like hell while they wait*"; or perhaps that old philosophical standby, "The harder I work, the luckier I get."

How easy leadership would be if employee ranks were filled with nothing but self-starters!

---

[1] *The Daily Oklahoman*, (August 23, 1987), p. 10. The Erma Bombeck column is syndicated nationwide by the *Los Angeles Times*.

Sorry. Would-be CEOs would expect frailty in others, and complacency is only one of the forms it takes. Another is just plain fear, and it comes in at least two flavors:

1. *Fear of embarrassment among peers.* The self-satisfied clerk is reluctant to make a suggestion that would enhance his or her importance to the organization for fear he is unqualified to perform and fears the embarrassment of a setback in the eyes of co-workers.
2. *Fear of displeasing superiors.* The insecure vice-president thinks there are ways to enhance revenues, but the necessary outlay of expenses could impact earnings over the near term if it did not work, thereby labeling him- or herself as a "spendthrift" and unworthy of advancement.

Another way of expressing the point is, "Expect no more of human nature than you have a right to expect." That way, disappointments will be sustained without bitterness.

A DOWN-TO-EARTH TRUTH

The potent poison of complacency and fear in defeating motivation can hardly be overstated. In fact, the hopefully helpful hints that follow later in this chapter—as possible antidotes—will be utterly useless to those who fail to understand and respect these basic impediments. I borrow the words of Jeno Polucci, who expresses it a little differently: "*Anyone who meets a payroll knows that people who really want to work for you are about the scarcest thing in industry.*"[2]

You need not read further concerning motivation unless you genuinely understand that, to get employees to perform minimum duties, one need only *drive them*. To gain their top performance, one must inspire them to *drive themselves.*[2] Only a paltry few have mastered this crucial skill, and that is the down-to-earth truth that makes understanding motivation so vital to every executive. Author James J. Cribben reinforces the concept this way: "Better for

---

[2] James J. Cribben, *Effective Managerial Leadership* (New York: AMACOM, 1972), p. 140.

the executive to have two people who work with him than five who labor for him. The former will multiply his productivity; the latter will merely drain his resources."[3]

LET'S CALL IT "INWARD MARKETING"

Until the mid-1950s, banks generally were all "pushing" the same traditional services toward the same complacent banking public, having nowhere else to turn. With the advent of national credit cards and dramatic technological advancements impacting the payment system, as well as the competitive threat of "nonbank" embryos, lethargy in banking was gone forever.

In June 1970, President Nixon appointed the Hunt Commission on Financial Structure and Regulation to weigh these developments along with relevant laws and regulatory practices for the purpose of proposing appropriate changes to facilitate a more effective banking system. Long before the commission's findings were implemented—some have still not been adopted—demand for competent banking talent heated up markedly as leaders in the industry tried feverishly to anticipate future competitive staff needs. Salary levels moved sharply higher. Just what happened next is conjectural, but in some banks *incentive compensation* was almost immediately born. One theory is that concerned bank directors from general industry (where this form of compensation had flourished for years) said, "Wait a bit. Rather than erode the bank's profit margin by a sharp increase in the general salary level, why not let the gains in pay be related to productivity?"

In record time, a variety of bonus formulas sprang up in banking, and by the early 1970s most money centers and large regional banks were rewarding their senior staff with from 10 to 50 percent of total compensation in the form of extra pay related to productivity, or what now is known as *incentive compensation*. In those early days the productivity was gauged almost entirely at the bottom line. Gradually, with the assistance of consultants, more creative variations emerged. Hay Management Associates[4] eventually advocated to some of its banking clients a *threefold approach:*

[3] Ibid.
[4] Management consultants, Philadelphia, 1973.

- Type A—related to predetermined *individual* goals;
- Type B—related to predetermined *departmental* goals; and
- Type C—related to predetermined growth objectives in *consolidated net income*.

For simplicity's sake, some Hay clients opted for only Type A and Type C, while a few others elected to go with only Types B and C. And within certain departments, straight commissions were introduced.

The author observed the Type A approach was the most productive, but also produced the most trauma. At first, some veteran officers were not at all certain how they felt about "sticking their necks out" for extra pay, when the downside might mean humiliation or even demotion. In those institutions where the very top executives (CEO included) were declaring 15 to 20 personal goals per year for themselves, others' attitudes soon became positive, and they did "stick their necks out." In fact, a few fell on their noses, but it quickly became clear that some *real personal growth* was taking place, especially when a strong effort was made to *quantify* the goals so that results could be measured more accurately at year-end.

In a 1985 business development monograph, the author dubbed this historic phenomenon "INWARD MARKETING." I trust its last two paragraphs will convey my intended meaning:

> The longer I remain involved with bank marketing, the more I realize that the most successful among us will be those who help others in their organizations achieve his or her own brand of success. Marketing executives who become totally preoccupied with customer need, product design, cost and pricing, advertising, or sales training—and these are vital—but fail to take the *inward look* at those within the organization who hunger to be shown how to grow more productive, may be doomed to mediocrity and, in some cases, failure.
>
> In short, *inward marketing plus incentive compensation equals leadership;* and the rewards of the current era in which banking finds itself will go to those who understand this powerful, introspective concept best and already have it in place. Indeed, it is difficult to conceive of any other concept or era that will ever supplant it.[5]

---

[5] J. W. McLean, "How CEO Led a Sales Evolution That Doubled Deposits," *Bank Marketing* (October 1985).

IN BOLD PERSPECTIVE

It was in 1913 that an obscure but brilliant math professor wrote on a blackboard in Austria, $E = MC^2$—a formula of immense scientific impact—that led to the harnessing of atomic power.

Thirty-two years later, when President Truman authorized the bombing of Japan to end World War II, Albert Einstein's earlier discovery that *energy equals mass times the speed of light squared* had changed the world.

In the world of motivation, the formula $IM + IC = L$ (in the author's admittedly highly biased opinion) has the potential for revolutionizing that esoteric world as well. Too bold, you say? Probably. In any event, *inward marketing plus incentive compensation equals leadership* has already demonstrated impressive results in comparison with more traditional approaches to motivation. The trick is how to make it happen.

SOME HOPEFULLY HELPFUL HINTS

When—and only when—the basic impediments to motivation and the principles of *inward marketing* are thoroughly recognized, the enlightened executive is then ready to consider *methods* that some have successfully employed to inspire and *empower* others to grow. This is not to say that all one needs is a formula or prescription for mastering such a subjective skill. Rather what follows are only five of the basic approaches that have yielded consistent results when pursued with care and patience:

1. *Declare their importance.* Nothing banishes fear more completely than for the individual to become convinced of his or her personal value in the overall mission of the group. An emotionally secure climate in the workplace—one that welcomes self expression—is essential before any other attempts to motivate superior performance can be truly effective. But the importance of their roles must be genuine. Insincerity (or even the erroneous perception of it) will be quickly resented and virtually seal off all subsequent efforts to achieve teamwork.

Precisely how and when to make the sincere declaration of a subordinate's importance will vary widely even within the same organization. Alternatives include:
- *Periodic evaluations of performance*—not less frequently than annually, please. Even quarterly is acceptable during the early phase of a new organizational thrust.
- *House organ articles*—which depict success stories of heretofore timid souls who dared to set difficult goals for themselves (tough pars as distinguished from easy bogeys) and how they overcame complacency and fear.
- *Local media coverage*—in the form of human interest profiles and feature articles concerning key employees, especially those who have overcome handicaps.

2. *Make it easy to try.* Who could object or feel threatened by a CEO who at the annual Christmas breakfast talks about individual career development and distributes a short questionnaire designed to facilitate personal goal setting for the new year (see figure 3). You might even offer a 5, 10, or 20 dollar bill at the exit door on the honor system to those who intend to turn in their completed questionnaire to their supervisor within 14 days or, in the alternative, surrender the currency (the books never balance on this, but who cares if lots of questionnaires come back!).

3. *Make it worthwhile to try.* Reward for trying can easily take two basic forms: (a) a *material stipend* (the amount is almost unimportant) at the end of the next year for those who excel and (b) *bring them up from the audience* next year for recognition before the entire staff for presentation of the material award, special seating, photograph, and *their remarks* (optional), etc.

Making it worthwhile to try can take many creative forms. Some years ago, a bank in Plano, Texas,[6] placed a bowl of quarters in front of each teller's window with a sign to the customer reading, "If this teller doesn't call you by name, take a quarter." At the end of each day, the teller got the quarters that were left—along with the *approbation* of the others if she led the pack.

[6] City National Bank, Earl S. Holland, president/CEO.

Some Hopefully Helpful Hints

ANNUAL CAREER DEVELOPMENT AND GOAL SETTING INVENTORY

THE GOAL OF BECOMING MORE EFFECTIVE PROFESSIONALLY CAN BE A REWARDING KEY TO PERSONAL GROWTH AND IS ALSO CENTRAL TO THE DEVELOPMENT AND CONTINUED SUCCESS OF LIBERTY. FOR BOTH OF THESE REASONS, WON'T YOU PLEASE TAKE THE TIME TO COMPLETE THIS QUESTIONNAIRE AND REFER IT TO YOUR SUPERVISOR FOR A CONFERENCE BY FRIDAY, JANUARY 16, 1987. THANK YOU.

J. W. McLEAN
SENIOR CHAIRMAN

		CIRCLE ONE	
1.	Did you give serious thought to the future development of your professional skills and productivity during this year?	YES	NO
2.	Did you consider how you might help reduce Liberty's expenses and/or enhance revenues?	YES	NO
3.	Did you discuss either of these subjects with your supervisor?	YES	NO
4.	Did your job involve new and enlarged responsibilities at any time during the year?	YES	NO
5.	Did you voluntarily learn a new professional skill during the year?	YES	NO
6.	Did you encourage someone else to learn a new professional skill during the year?	YES	NO
7.	Did you attempt to measure the results of your efforts to grow more skillful and productive, in order to set new goals for next year?	YES	NO

NOTE: Score yourself a grade of "C" for 3 yes answers; a "B" for 4 or 5 yes answers; and an "A" for 6 or 7 yes answers.

MY PERSONAL (OR GROUP) GOAL (OR GOALS) FOR THE NEW YEAR IS (ARE):

_____
_____
_____
_____

Signed: _____

Figure 3

It was in 1968 that the Dean of Professional Development at the University of Cincinnati, Dr. Phillip Marvin, wrote: "One of the myths of management is that men will do a better job if they are paid more money. It just is not true. Past experience points out that a man cannot be *paid* to do a better job, he must *want* to do a better job."[7]

I'm sure this is why the Plano bank gimmick worked so well with only quarters in the bowl.

4. *Explain how action often precedes motivation.* In the September 1987 *Reader's Digest,* a prominent motivational authority is quoted as saying, "Motivation rarely comes first, action does! You have to 'prime the pump.' If you wait until you're in the mood, you may wait forever."[8]

Who among us cannot recall it has often been *after* we get involved in a task that we only then become powerfully motivated? Indeed, the last six chapters of this book were much, much more easily outlined and written than the agonizing first four. Self-discipline is one of life's most formidable challenges—but thankfully it is habit forming. Further, one thing (maybe the only thing) on which psychologists agree is that we are at our best—physically and mentally—when we are disciplined, preferably by ourselves.

5. *Demonstrate by example.* How incomplete our "hopefully helpful hints" would be without this near-platitude. Quite obviously the "boss" must not only be involved personally, but also should have been involved with the goal-setting process for years in advance.

However commendable it may be of the chief executive to stress staff motivation for the sake of individual career development and personal growth, he also knows very well how crucial it is to the ongoing development of *earning power,* the all-important subject of the next chapter.

[7] Philip Marvin, *Management Goals, Guidelines and Accountability* (New York: Dow Jones-Irwin, Inc., 1968), p. 69.

[8] David D. Burns, M.D., *Feeling Good, the New Mood Therapy* (New York: Morrow Publishers, 1980).

Some privileged CEOs have also learned the exhilarating gratification that comes from a plain note of appreciation like this one quoted verbatim from the author's personal files—one of my most-valued trophies of 40 years in business:

> Just wanted to say thanks for your time and good relaxed visit.
> As usual, I came away with immediate food for thought and lots of input to draw from over the busy days ahead.
> After dispelling those negative thoughts I shared with you, I have pushed new positive ideas into the forefront.
> In other words, I've gotten off high center—
> Thanks to you.

THE SERENDIPITY EFFECT OF *EMPOWERING*

Upon reflection, *empowering others* through *inward marketing* has produced some quite unexpected results that deserve sharing here:

- While preparing for abdominal surgery, a safe deposit officer sold his anesthetist a money market account and, later, a large CD renewal relationship.
- A junior officer in the controller's division distinguished herself all year long by cross-selling IRAs and CDs to her credit card customers and graduated the next year to bring in six-figure money market accounts.
- Another busy data processing officer was cited for his persistence—on his own time—in attracting several high level customers, as the result of his taking pains to explore the pesonal banking needs of some suppliers.
- A usually shy operations officer skillfully converted a belligerent customer complaint into a new $300,000 CD and, as a result, the officer is now a regular business developer.
- A central file officer, having virtually no customer contact on her job, became a leading cross-selling winner, simply by translating otherwise bland filing data into business development prospects.

MOTIVATION AT ITS BEST?

Yes, indeed. In fact, the author confesses that such examples also serve as powerful REVERSE-MOTIVATION in terms of their resounding reconfirmation that painstaking effort to empower others is not an idle exercise.

ARE THERE NO INCENTIVE PLAN PITFALLS?

Kindly restrain your euphoria concerning motivation through goal setting and incentive compensation. There are some formidable *pitfalls* that, hopefully, can be minimized by the following straightforward warnings:

Warning No. 1: There will almost invariably be someone who feels (whether she says so or not) that individual goals are not uniformly difficult nor is the incentive compensation *equitable* among participants. Quite unfortunately, they will be right. Complete uniformity and total equality are fanciful myths. It is far better to acknowledge these shortcomings at the outset as the group "crosses the threshhold" along with a good faith commitment to compensate for such discrepancies during the next period.

The author recalls that several early incentive compensation plan years produced genuine protests by some of the most productive executives—those with direct customer related duties—who thought their Type A goals were tougher than the more general tasks of some of their peers. But time and performance ultimately made the process more equitable.

Warning No. 2: No matter how thorough the process, effective goal setting can never be infallible or even complete for very long. The mere passage of 30 days can usher in an entirely new set of more pertinent ones. Moreover, failure to introduce *interim objectives* for too long a period can result in your most productive people going through an entire year with their eyes "on the wrong ball." Indeed, incentive compensation that leaves no room for mid-course correction could well prove to be counterproductive.

The author remembers well the suddenness with which his bank's policy toward energy loans changed in 1982. The plunge in world oil prices introduced entirely new initiatives on the part of loan officers and bold "mid-course corrections" had to be made in incentive compensation goals, the new emphasis being on credit liquidation rather than more credit extension.

Warning No. 3: Almost any incentive plan, unless it is sadly deficient, can become a *monitoring nightmare*. Because effective goal setting must be a participative process, the scoring mechanics at the end of the period necessarily will require joint involvement. This, of course, can be traumatic in the closing days of a busy period, especially year-end, when the sheer weight of the number of people involved can frustrate the whole effort. It will be particularly so during the early years.

The author will long remember that very first incentive compensation plan year and the unexpected pressures associated with the initial scoring and closing process, which literally reached a frenzy peak in late December 1972. Some of the frustration was, of course, self inflicted by unfamiliarity with the system and a basic insecurity about the whole thing. But fortunately we had resisted Hay Associates' three-level format: (1) individual goals; (2) departmental goals; and (3) organizational goals. We had opted only for numbers 1 and 3, and that was certainly complex enough for the first year. I dread to think of the consequences had we attempted all three levels during any of those early years.

Rendering a completely fair scorecard during a stressful period is an enormous challenge and, if not understood, can amount to a costly pitfall indeed.

A CONCLUDING NOTE

Building a sales culture takes years. Likewise, successful "inward marketing" requires both *precious time and limitless patience* on the part of the key motivators. Meanwhile, the SUPERVISOR'S PRAYER by John Luther seems to put it all in clear perspective:

DEAR LORD, PLEASE HELP ME—
  TO ACCEPT HUMAN BEINGS AS THEY ARE—
    NOT YEARN FOR PERFECT CREATURES;
  TO RECOGNIZE ABILITY—AND ENCOURAGE IT;
  TO UNDERSTAND SHORTCOMINGS—AND MAKE
    ALLOWANCE FOR THEM;
  TO WORK PATIENTLY FOR IMPROVEMENT—
    AND NOT EXPECT TOO MUCH TOO QUICKLY;
  TO APPRECIATE WHAT PEOPLE DO RIGHT—
    NOT JUST CRITICIZE WHAT THEY DO WRONG;
  TO BE SLOW TO ANGER AND HARD TO
    DISCOURAGE;
  TO HAVE THE HIDE OF AN ELEPHANT AND
    THE PATIENCE OF JOB;
  IN SHORT, LORD, PLEASE HELP ME BE A
    BETTER BOSS.[9]

Being a better boss has also been summed up in just four words. They are not mine. I wish they were. It was Rear Admiral Grace Hopper, USN (Ret.), who said:

"MANAGE THINGS, LEAD PEOPLE."[10]

Earning power—the subject of the next chapter—will be understood best against this background.

---

[9] John Luther, *Soundings* (Fairfield, N.J., The Economics Press, Inc., March, 1987).

[10] T. Boone Pickins, Jr., *Boone* (Boston: Houghton Mifflin Company, 1987), p. 273.

Chapter 5

UNDERSTANDING EARNING POWER

Take one eye off the bottom line and you may as well close both.
—Anonymous

EARNING POWER DOESN'T JUST HAPPEN

In this chapter, we will build our understanding of earning power upon the bedrock principle that all else depends first upon the building of an organization-wide *marketing culture*. Next, we will note how the Master Planning Model (MPM) introduced in Chapter 2 and each of its FIVE STEPS is an ideal template for developing and enhancing earning power. Then, under STEP 4. Implementation, we will discover that the "art of (?) selling" is not an *art* at all but rather a *skill* that can be learned through the mastery of both *people knowledge* (their basic needs, that is, the Maslow Pyramid) and *product knowledge,* with some basic exploratory techniques for implementing each effectively. The chapter closes with a fresh perspective on some old bromides in the corporate world that either can be easily overdone or no longer apply: (a) "Always kneel at the shrine of superior customer service"; (b) "save those dog locations"; (c) "don't be too obviously commercial"; and (d) "go for hi-tech, whatever the cost." Each of these myths will be debunked in our quest of *maximum sustainable earning power*—through a patiently nurtured organization-wide *marketing culture,* led by the chief executive officer. It really doesn't just happen.

A PERCEPTIVE QUESTION—OR JUST A TRICKY ONE?

Once or twice a year, as far back as I can remember, it was most stimulating to host an orientation luncheon for the new officers. After dining and normal preliminaries, I would ask the group to think with me for a moment on the question, "What is the *purpose* of a business—any business?" Invariably the consensus response, in so many words, would be, "To make a profit."

"NOT SO!" I would say respectfully.

And then I would go on and submit for the group's consideration the proposition that "the enlightened purpose of any business should be *to solve customer problems,* from which profits would most assuredly be the result."

Understanding how generating earning power, FIRST, means a commitment to problem solving, and, *SECOND,* how to harness the necessary resources and talents to sustain it for the long term— together—will be the subject of this chapter. No chief executive can function very well or for very long, in my view, without these key concepts clearly and uppermost in mind.

BUGGY WHIP SALES OFF AGAIN THIS YEAR

The historical toll of product obsolescence is all too well known in industry; witness the demise of the proverbial buggy whip. Yet how blindly loyal managers can be to their particular product or service despite all else, and how sadly this phenomenon remains a leading cause of death in both manufacturing and service industries.

In a single generation the heavy passenger use of railroad travel has yielded mightily to the airliner; scores of patent medicines have given way to antibiotics and other medical triumphs; and scarcely any product or service for sale today was available in precisely its present form only a few years ago.

Yes, the ravenous customer reigns supreme—not the ever-changing product or service—and nothing happens in the earnings column until the customer buys. But continuity of sales is utterly dependent on the seller's consistently winning out with the customer against two major foes:

1. Other *perceptive sellers*
2. *The customers' fickle needs, wants, desires,* and—oh yes—*new problems to be solved*

Regrettably there are still some business executives and many salespeople who are not aware of the distinction between what they sell and what their customers buy. What is sold, to be sure, are goods and services, but what is bought are benefits: It is warmth, not gas; it is light, not electricity; it is vision, not glasses; it is entertainment, not the television set, and so forth.

Nor do women buy makeup. They buy the expectation that they will look and feel more attractive to others. As Revlon founder Charles Revson once said, "In the factory we make cosmetics. In the store we sell hope."[1]

BUT WHO WINS A TIE?

What we have really been talking about is how inextricably entwined earning power is with selling solutions to problems, and there is a discipline—indeed a science—that pulls it all together: *marketing*. But *selling and marketing are not synonymous*. It has been said that a great *salesperson* can sell ice cubes to Eskimos, but a great *marketer* would not. Similarly, true marketing philosophy holds that there is no winner or loser in an ideal sales situation—both buyer and seller must benefit. A great *salesperson* produces impressive revenues. A great *marketer* creates profitable customer relationships that endure. When you are the customer and the products are identical, which would you prefer to patronize: the *salesperson* or the *marketer*? In terms of your own long-term benefit, there is really no contest, is there?

[1] *Soundings* vol. 3, no. 12 (1987), p. 14.

In baseball, a tie goes to the runner. In customer relations, *a tie goes to the marketer,* the one whose product or service has the added value of being offered by a genuine, caring counselor, as distinguished from a glib, calculating order-taker. It is known as the "value-added" concept of marketing. This principle was beautifully demonstrated not long ago by my oldest son. By the time this is published, I trust he will not mind too much my sharing this one anecdotal experience, which also amounts to a prime example of what Larry Wilson[2] calls *counselor selling.*

Larry McLean found himself in what appeared to be a tie in bidding for his firm (a major Wall Street house) on the management of a $50 million money market fund, which would lead to still more business over time. All the "majors" were after it, and the bids were almost indistinguishable. A "people guy" with both an MBA and a CPA, Larry got the business! When asked how it happened, he said, "I'm really not sure, but our solving one of their computer problems at the time didn't hurt us any."

Need more be said on behalf of the relationship between *problem solving* and *earning power?* Indeed, it is a key marketing tool for achieving *maximum sustainable long-range earning power,* and it leads us to the *basic approach* any organization should follow in order to harness the necessary resources and talents to make it all happen.

BUILDING A MARKETING CULTURE

Seasoned chief executives know very well that problem solving works best in an organization-wide marketing culture, but they also know that they have no monopoly on marketing philosophy any more than their companies are the exclusive providers of superior products or services. They know, too, that capturing a loyal customer base does not just happen. Marketing experts have told us for years that at least three factors are involved. Listed alphabetically, they are:

- convenience

---

[2] The founder of Wilson Learning Company and a prominent sales training expert, currently in Santa Fe.

- price
- service

Writing in *American Banker,* consultant Jack Whittle recently stated that "customers won by good service will remain the most loyal." He continued, "The worst possible situation for a bank occurs when the customer designates price as the No. 1 factor in choosing a bank, convenience as No. 2, and service last as No. 3." Whittle's thesis holds that *pricing* competition is the most expensive for a bank to deliver, while *service* competition is the least costly to maintain over time. "The ideal situation is to have customers who say that they bank where they bank primarily because of service, followed by convenience and then by price."[3]

The best point-of-sale ad I ever saw was a placard in a barber shop. It read, "Our dandruff remover shampoo costs twice as much as our closest competitor's. If it does not remove your dandruff, we'll give you twice your money back."

If it all sounds too easy, why not just raise all your prices and advertise your superior service? HOLD IT. You dare not even think about such a strategy until you have achieved a genuine marketing culture throughout the ranks of your staff all across the organization. Such minor details as *perceptive hiring, sales training* (much more on this later), *motivation with incentives* (a slow walk back through Chapter 4 might be in order here), *setting goals and quotas, measuring results,* and *openly rewarding top achievers*—all these need to come first.

When a business, particularly a service-oriented business, can never hope to achieve significant product distinction, *institutional distinction* is the only acceptable marketing alternative, and building its marketing culture is the most direct route to adding value to its otherwise indistinguishable products.

RESEARCH REVISITED

Back in Chapter 3, RESEARCH was proposed as STEP 1 in any worthy management effort, which certainly includes the development of earning power. Clearly no set of earnings goals—STEP

---

[3] September 2, 1987. Mr. Whittle is chairman of Whittle & Hanks, Inc., Chicago.

2—would be realistic or reliable unless based on an assessment of:

- coming economic conditions;
- likely competitive market pressures; and
- organizational competence.

The author agrees with Yogi Berra that, "You can observe a lot by watching." And when it comes to achieving *maximum sustainable long-range earning power,* research is absolutely essential. Furthermore, in case you are still unconvinced, Kenneth Fisher advocates the avoidance of investing in any company that spends less than one-fifteenth of its aggregate market value on research annually. He constructs a price/research ratio (PRR) and suggests that super companies of the future will be found among those which have PRRs between five and ten today.[4]

WHICH WAY IS NORTH?

Back in Chapter 2, GOAL SETTING was proposed as STEP 2. Even vague objectives are worthwhile in terms of clarifying direction. Too many businesses today are incapable of identifying their primary direction for more than a few weeks at a time, that is, which products, which services, which markets will be featured, which will be deemphasized? But earnings objectives worth their salt really should be both quantified and well beyond easy reach. It is generally accepted that the most convenient and effective way to do this is to organize the whole effort according to:

- short-term goals (12 months)
- medium-term goals (2 to 4 years)
- long-term goals (5 plus years).

A reminder is in order. As suggested in Chapter 2, even the best performing organizations have need of structural changes from time to time, in order to clarify accountability and authority. Such

---

[4] Kenneth Fisher, CEO and founder, Fisher Investments, Burlingame, California, reported by *USA Today* (September 13, 1984), p. 38.

needs deserve the highest priority—let's call them urgent goals—if earnings goals are to be meaningful.

Finally, the dedicated CEO must never forget that the organization's future revenues and ultimate earnings destination—its monetary goals—can never amount to more than the sum total of each department's marketing goals; and these, in turn, can be no more than the composite sales goals of individuals.

NO CREDIT FOR "WINDFALL" EARNINGS

In establishing earnings objectives for a public company, there is sometimes the temptation to capitalize on a one-time earnings opportunity. Nonrecurring profits, however, will be quickly detected by security analysts and "stripped out" of their calculations in projecting the real earning power of the business. This is not to say that such erratic gains are undesirable and always to be avoided. Not at all; only that they should either be used to establish reserves or, at least, reported as "extraordinary." Indeed, all of this is simply to stress the desirability of a MASTER GOAL of striving for MAXIMUM SUSTAINABLE LONG-RANGE EARNING POWER.

The key word here is "sustainable."

PLANNING IS THE CENTERPIECE, BUT NOT ALL THERE IS

Back in Chapter 2, PLANNING was proposed as STEP 3. Quantified earnings goals, even those based on careful and comprehensive research, are for naught without a clear-cut set of plans fixing individual responsibility. WHO is going to do WHAT? . . . WHEN? . . . and HOW? The 12-month horizon is known in most organizations as the *profit plan*. The 2- to 4-year horizon is generally referred to as the *business plan*.

In many businesses, PLANNING is thought to be an end in itself. It is my studied conclusion, however, that planning is only the centerpiece—STEP 3—of a five-step process. RESEARCH and GOAL SETTING are STEPS 1 and 2, with IMPLEMENTATION and MONITORING RESULTS being STEPS 4 and 5.

In sum, planning *can* make the difference between an organization on the move and one that drifts. But planning *cannot* be more than a superficial exercise without:

research and goal setting preceding it
and
implementation and monitoring results following.

IF YOU WOULD WALK ON WATER, YOU MUST GET OUT OF THE BOAT

Back in Chapter 2, IMPLEMENTATION was proposed as STEP 4. IMPLEMENTATION is the clincher in most master planning endeavors. When earning power is at stake, it calls for a lot of plain talk with staff concerning THE ART (?) OF SELLING.

Is selling really an art or talent in the sense that one must be born with it? Not if you believe the thousands of successful salesmen who have told how they learned to sell just as they learned any other skill. In fact, approaching selling as an art is the number one barrier to success. Why? Simply because most people know they do not have the special artistic talent and are therefore defeated before they even try to sell.

The dictionary tells us, "A *skill* is an ability that comes from knowledge and practice." Therefore, if selling is not something one is blessed with at birth, what does that tell us? That's right. IT CAN BE LEARNED.

Earlier in this chapter, it was suggested that when a sale is made what the buyer buys is a solution to a problem. Now, if we are going to be skillful at helping people solve problems with our product (or service), what kinds of knowledge must we have? The obvious answer: We need both PRODUCT KNOWLEDGE and PEOPLE KNOWLEDGE.

Knowing the product (or service) means many things, depending on its sophistication and technical features. But in addition to all its characteristics, remember the benefit of "added value." YOU as "counselor" rather than mere "salesman" are an invaluable ingredient in any sale situation.

If You Would Walk on Water, You Must Get Out of the Boat

People knowledge means understanding their needs. An eminent psychologist at Brandeis University, Abraham H. Maslow, taught that there are certain needs basic to all of us, and in fact they form an interesting pyramid (see figure 4) that the reader perhaps has already encountered elsewhere. Maslow held that at the broad base of the pyramid is the greatest and most prevalent need of all: the need for *physical comfort* (the relatively basic needs which in today's world have become necessities). Next, as the sides of the pyramid pinch in, comes the need for *security* (a job or profession that provides economic stability). Next, the need for *social acceptance* (the inborn desire in each of us to "belong"). Then comes *personal esteem*, according to Maslow (the strong need in each of us

THE MASLOW PYRAMID OF NEEDS

SELF-ACTUALIZATION
(need to be all we can be)

PERSONAL ESTEEM
(need to like ourselves)

SOCIAL ACCEPTANCE
(need to belong)

SECURITY
(economic)

PHYSICAL COMFORT
(basic necessities)

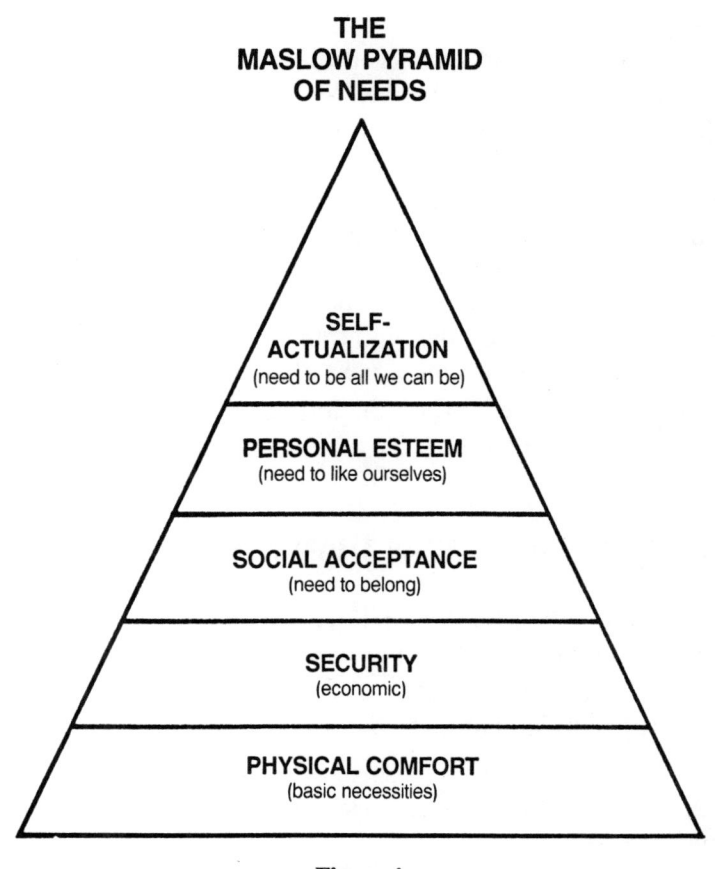

Figure 4

to "like ourselves" free of guilt and torturous failures); and then, finally, at the very top of the Maslow pyramid we find *self-actualization* (the strongest need in each of us—once the basic ones are filled—the need to be all we can be).[5]

Against this background the perceptive sales counselor will seek to learn which of the basic needs is having the greatest influence on the prospect at the time. Here are four exploratory techniques that have proven useful:

First, ASK QUESTIONS to establish facts and to establish feelings.

Second, UNCOVER OBJECTIONS; no amount of time is too great to deal with objections.

Third, counter with FEEL/FELT/FOUND.[6] If you can do so with credibility, let the prospect know that "You know how she FEELS. . . ." "Others FELT the same way . . . until they FOUND how your product solved the problem."

Fourth, use the MINIMAX METHOD. Show how there is MINIMUM risk to explore the possibilities of MAXIMUM gain, that is, "Try it at our expense . . . nothing really to lose." This is one of the most powerful of all sales techniques.

The only purpose here is to make the indelible point that achievement of earnings goals inevitably requires group implementation of well-laid plans that fix responsibility for business development targets with a timetable, and that calls for selling. Sales do not happen without sales training, and that effort is of questionable value unless customer problem solving becomes a way of life throughout the organization.

A SCORECARD GIVES MORE THAN THE SCORE

Back in Chapter 2, MONITORING RESULTS was proposed as STEP 5. Obviously in order to reward exemplary performance, the results of sales efforts must be carefully monitored, fairly evaluated (with appropriate adjustment for joint efforts), accurately tabu-

---

[5] A. H. Maslow "A Theory of Human Motivation," *Psychological Review* (1943), pp. 370–396.

[6] Wilson Learning Company, Minneapolis, a banking seminar, San Francisco, 1964.

lated, lovingly disseminated, and promptly rewarded. Anything less will only frustrate and eventually stifle participation. It is hard enough to get the staff involved; do not let a sloppy monitoring system drag the whole effort down. As one of baseball's most vocal managers has said, "Unless you play to win, why bother to keep the score?"[7]

Of equal (if not more) importance are at least three additional aspects of clean, clear scorekeeping that are sometimes overlooked:

1. Early knowledge of interim results of a sales campaign and its effect on earnings—even when disappointing—can often become the basis for a MID-COURSE CORRECTION which, in time may have a dramatic effect on final results.
2. This knowledge also provides a solid basis for making incentive compensation awards.
3. Whatever the results, they will provide the finest kind of RESEARCH when you are ready to repeat the whole process over again—STEPS 1 through 5—especially when new goals are set for the next period.

THE SHRINE OF SUPERIOR CUSTOMER SERVICE

As a means of achieving *maximum sustainable long-range earning power,* the author has delivered scores of staff sermons over the years on the absolute necessity of providing *superior customer service.* Like anything else, however, even allegiance to superior service can be overdrawn. Better to err on that side, of course, but it is quite possible for businesses to become what Booz-Allen & Hamilton[8] calls "chronic observers." These firms almost always think they are guilty of poor service.

Banks are prime examples. At a 1987 banking conference on cost control, the consulting firm revealed that 64 percent of branch customers surveyed never waited a second; 72 percent waited less than 30 seconds; and almost all were served within a minute. Booz-Allen & Hamilton also reported that, whereas most customers

---

[7] Billy Martin, New York Yankees, "Today Show," April 1987.
[8] Management consultants, Chicago.

hardly waited at all, a substantial segment would have been satisfied to wait up to 10 minutes to make a deposit.

The conference conclusion[9] was that too often banks allowed their staffing and service levels to be dictated by anecdote ("Old Mrs. Jones once had to wait 15 minutes") rather than by sound data, and that many could confidently reduce service levels and cut expenses without a measurable increase in consumer dissatisfaction.

Expense control, of course, is an enormous subject in itself involving a tough group budgeting process and periodic accountability tests. But missing earnings goals by "kneeling too long at the shrine" of superior customer service can and should be consciously avoided.

TEXACO LEARNED BETTER

Seated quietly on a coast-to-coast flight some years ago (I believe about 1966), I had a seatmate who observed that I was reading a marketing piece, and he introduced himself as director of marketing for Texaco. Because I then held the same office at Bank of America, we were amused by the coincidence and proceeded for the next two hours to engage in a lively discussion about our respective jobs and their remarkable similarities. One point I shall never forget: in those days Texaco was advertising prominently that it served all 50 states. In fact, it was the first of the giant oil companies to attempt this. Because Bank of America was then the largest bank in the world, with more than a thousand branches in California alone, we naturally focused immediately on the operational headaches that go with far-flung locations.

It was during this part of our absorbing visit that he asked, "Would you care to guess what my toughest problem is these days?" I am not sure what I volunteered. Perhaps something about staffing, which was our constant nemesis at B of A. He was nice enough to say I was partly correct, but that his toughest problem turned out to be what he termed "his dog locations": those service stations that seemed to continue to deteriorate in profitability, no matter what was done to turn them around. He then said, "Several times lately we've put our best operators in our worst locations, and

---

[9] As reported by Sanford Rose in *American Banker* (December 22, 1987).

before long we lose them both." He then explained how they had learned this bitter lesson too many times and how they no longer hesitated to close "dog locations."

What a sermonette on enlightened marketing.

In later years I heard the same principle expressed another way by a prominent banker (no less). My old friend Chuck McCoy of Baton Rouge, Louisiana, once told me: "I have been so busy putting out fires . . . that I have been unable to start one."

HOW COMMERCIAL CAN YOU GET?

Well, when is it permissible to spend money to make money? How long should a business development effort take to prove itself worthy? When is payday?

Some of the liveliest arguments I have ever witnessed have revolved around these almost unanswerable questions. Indeed, I doubt if any two individuals would agree completely on a half dozen specific examples of trading off expense dollars for future revenue.

However, I will cite one business development ploy—purely conceived in good will—about which there is absolutely no doubt as to its ultimate payday. Indeed, within a matter of days each year we attempted it there was a surprise windfall of new business. I am referring to what I used to call our FATHER AND SON LUNCHEONS. Each year between Christmas and New Year's Day, the customer contact officers and I would host a luncheon for college-age sons (returning home from school) and their dads. Sure, it took some fairly elaborate planning and it was not inexpensive. Except for those three years in California, I watched the thing firsthand from 1950 to 1986—and it really worked. There was nothing like it in terms of generating customer loyalty or breaking through the toughest prospect's resistance.

OF COURSE IT WAS COMMERCIAL! It was so stated at each luncheon:

> Gentlemen, I have a confession to make. We invite you here each year very selfishly. It's entirely too easy to lose track of you once you go away to college for four, five, and perhaps six years— and those are just the undergraduate years for some of you (ha ha). We really want to get to know you as well as we know your dads—

and that's saying an awful lot in some cases (ha ha). So you are the program here today. Please stand and give us your name, campus, how you're classified (freshman, sophomore, junior, or senior) plus anything you might wish to tell us about your father (ha ha).

And so they did, year after year, and the new accounts rolled in along with some fine new recruits for our training program. The flaw, of course, was the absence of mothers and daughters, but that's another story—and a very deserving one.

HI-TECH: AN EARNINGS PLUS OR MINUS?

More than 40 years ago in Murray Hill, New Jersey, Bell Telephone Laboratories conducted the first demonstration of human voice amplification by an unlikely contraption, later to become known as a transistor, and a new age in technology was born. Its importance has grown as rapidly as its size has diminished. Today transistors are the core elements of radios, televisions, telephone systems, pacemakers, compact disc instruments, and, of course, computers.

The early generation of computers built without transistors filled large rooms and required large service teams just to replace the vacuum tubes that blew out with expensive regularity. They were also slower than today's pocket calculators. The story of how inventing the transistor involved the experimental use of silicon and required jumping a series of intellectual hurdles is a fascinating one that serves no real purpose here—except to illustrate the magnitude of technological change and the enormity of its potential impact on our daily lives.

Walter Wriston wrote in *Forbes:*

> Today, there are more than 200,000 computer screens in hundreds of trading rooms, in dozens of countries, which light up to display an unending flow of news. . . . Every government in the world is filing a kind of continually updated global 10-K about its economic health. . . . Global markets are a kind of free speech. . . ."[10]

[10] Walter Wriston, former chairman and CEO of Citicorp, New York City, "A New Kind of Free Speech," *Forbes* (December 14, 1987), p. 119.

But what does—or should—technological change mean to the typical business? How technologically innovative should a business be?

There can be little doubt that ignoring technological advancement can be a costly—if not fatal—mistake. New ways of bringing technology-based products and services to market have usually paid handsome rewards to the *leader*. Unfortunately, however, we can only guess how many *followers* have failed at the game and suffered the high financial toll of attempting in vain to build a truly competitive technology workforce. Further, turnover in the middle executive ranks of technicians continues to present an increasingly difficult challenge (20 percent annually is a minimum) with salary jumps more frequent than for others, producing severe administrative headaches.

As in most business decisions, technological generalizations are useless. Whether pursuit of technology is or is not for you and your firm, then, can only be answered by a completely objective assessment of how you might use it to (a) create new products, or (b) deliver old ones more profitably.

There is an old anonymous saying that *"there can be much too much of a good thing. For instance, throwing one end of a rope to a person who has broken through the ice on a lake is good. Throwing both ends is much too much."*

"INWARD MARKETING" REVISITED

In the preceding chapter, the concept of "inward marketing" was advanced as a means of inspiring greater staff productivity by relating bonus compensation to the attainment of predetermined goals, that is, turning the marketing thrust first inward which, in turn, almost surely will broaden the outward effectiveness of the customer problem-solving effort.

And so it goes.

In pursuit of greater earning power, of course diligent expense control, periodic audit, and a careful overview of all operations should have highest priorities. But—more and more, as I reflect on business triumphs and failures of the past—I AM THOROUGHLY CONVINCED THAT THE KEY TO MOST EARNINGS PROBLEMS IS *NEW*

BUSINESS DEVELOPMENT, AND IT WORKS BEST IN A FERTILE *MARKETING CULTURE*—SPAWNED AND PATIENTLY NURTURED BY THE CHIEF EXECUTIVE OFFICER.

Of course, it does not hurt a bit if it is also embraced by an enlightened directorate and a representative number of major shareholders, one of the issues we will probe in Chapter 6.

Chapter 6

UNDERSTANDING BOARD AND SHAREHOLDER RELATIONSHIPS

Good times breed friends—tough times test them.
—Anonymous

WE'RE NOW TALKING JOB SECURITY

This will be one of the book's shortest chapters, not because its subject matter is unimportant but rather because the dynamics of a chief executive's involvement with directors and owners of the business are not really very complicated. Indeed, one page could have summed it up—and perhaps even a single word, COMMUNICATIONS, says it all.

Why?

Simply because the CEO has more bosses than anyone else on the payroll, and failure to recognize and genuinely accept their crucial roles and perceive their points of view will almost certainly insure an ineffective—if not brief—tenure. Indeed, a CEO's very livelihood, no matter what other qualifications he brings to the job, is directly dependent upon the level of communications skills he is able to develop and practice on a daily basis with both directors and owners alike. In this respect, there is little difference between directors and owners, perhaps only the frequency of contact.

AS A CEO, YOU *WORK* FOR THEM. THEY *DO NOT WORK* FOR YOU. Always remember, too, that, not unlike Notre Dame football fans, they are with you WIN or TIE! If this is an overdrawn indictment, it also happens to be the CEO's safest assumption.

SOME CARDINAL COMMANDMENTS

In approximate chronological order (but not necessarily in order of importance), here are TEN COMMANDMENTS for fulfilling the CEO's fundamental communications priorities:

1. THOU SHALT DEMONSTRATE YOUR PERSONAL DEDICATION TO THE JOB. Do not let them have reason to doubt your "25 hour" commitment, consistent always with a common sense approach toward effective performance without debilitating stress or fatigue consequences (more on this subject in Chapter 10). Every directorate has its overly cautious skeptics who genuinely believe their mission in corporate life is to "keep management on its toes." *Your assignment:* perform consistently in such a dedicated manner that keeping you "on your toes" is quite all right, but "pushing you off balance" is neither appropriate nor acceptable.

2. THOU SHALT RECOMMEND AND CAUSE THE ESTABLISHMENT OF BASIC POLICIES. A good point of departure might well be a redefinition of the company's mission statement:
    - What is its *purpose?*
    - What are its *objectives?*
    - Are its *efforts* consistent with them?
    - How often should the mission statement be reviewed?

Such a beginning should logically lead to a complete review of the BYLAWS, which, of course, should involve counsel along with qualified outside members of the board. Good models are easily available for setting forth required functions and key relationships between:
    - Shareholders
    - Directors
    - Various committees

Some Cardinal Commandments

- The chief executive
- Other officers
- The general staff.

An *executive committee* (or its equivalent) is also strongly recommended if only to consider matters of *major policy* between meetings of the board. Such a provision will, however, be no more effective than your definition of *major policy* and the degree of the directors' agreement as to its meaning.

3. THOU SHALT NOT LET THEM GUESS AT THE NUMBERS. No suspense concerning periodic earnings, please. Nothing will inspire doubts about your management competence sooner than irregular or inaccurate earnings reporting, even if the final results are otherwise acceptable. Delegation of this or any other function does not remove the CHIEF from direct accountability. The dictionary itself defines "chief" as "one who authorizes, controls and supervises the acts of others." Financial reporting must be accurate, prompt, thorough, and consistent, or the director/shareholder will have legitimate ground for complaint (or worse).

4. THOU SHALT QUICKLY ANNOUNCE BAD NEWS. No *cover-ups,* please, even if you are tempted to wait for what you feel almost certainly will temper or offset its effect. The CEO must be accountable for every hour between the moment of knowledge and the time it is shared with appropriate parties. It is equally essential to be absolutely certain that every development of significance to the director/owner is disclosed fully. The safest rule to follow here is: When in doubt, GO PUBLIC. Our subtitle of Chapter 10 also works well here: "Nothing is as bad as you thought it would be—or as good." But even if it is worse, you still have no choice.

    In commenting on the CEO's duty to *full disclosure* and its possible short-term negative effect on directors, a wise and renowned corporate leader, Jack Abernathy, once said to me, "Bill, better to make them *sullen* than *rebellious!*"[1]

5. THOU SHALT NOT BE SHY ABOUT TELLING THE GOOD STUFF. Some chief executives literally do become so

---

[1] Jack Abernathy served the Big Chief Drilling Company of Oklahoma City in various capacities from 1946 to 1981, when he retired as Chairman.

paranoid, so uncomfortable with the media and the security analysts that they miss numerous perfectly legitimate opportunities to put their *"best foot forward."* In fact, when an unforeseen development is likely to influence future earning power favorably, your counsel would probably point out that failure to disclose can be every bit as condemning as exaggeration or fabrication of the news.

6. THOU SHALT LET THEM KNOW HOW THEY CAN HELP; THEN DEMAND IT. In earlier days, some directors and shareholders enjoyed a uniquely privileged status, one that was "above" business development or customer contact. Those days are over in most business enterprises, which are all the better for it. Of course, the other extreme—a meddlesome director/owner—can outweigh the positive effects of those who discharge their duties in an organized way. In any case, every director should have one or more *active* committee assignments with a meaningful scope of work and periodic reporting requirements.

7. THOU SHALT SEEK WAYS TO REWARD AND DISTINGUISH THEM. It is the CEO's responsibility not only to orchestrate the board's involvement with both management and marketing functions, but also to sustain it over time through creative incentives. One such innovation was the CONTRIBUTORS PROGRAM at Oklahoma's largest bank (introduced when the bank was "trying harder" in second place); it was so named because the array of awards for successful business development efforts took the form of cash donations to the performing director's favorite nonprofit agency. Research had disclosed that directors had no interest in cash or merchandise for themselves, while recognition as philanthropists provided a unique appeal.

8. THOU SHALT NOT INDULGE IN MEDIA OVERKILL. Publicity is a seductive potion. Few among us can resist being asked for our opinion on a public issue or some aspect of the business we know best. There are, however, at least two significant risks:
    a. The chance that an impromptu reply will look less than professional in print.

Never Mind the "Build-up" 75

b. The chance that a too-frequent exposure will render one's comments ineffective over time.
Far better results are achieved when media requests are dealt with more deliberately and the "call-back" technique is employed, even if only a few minutes are gained for composing a more thoughtful response. *A CEO is judged very strictly by his public utterances*—and indeed he should be.

9. THOU SHALT NOT HESITATE TO "WORRY 'EM" ABOUT THEIR LEGAL EXPOSURE. Although most directors know they can be sued for their corporate decisions, many still are not aware of how exposed they can be, depending upon the terms of their director and officer (D&O) insurance coverage. Most display an extremely low awareness of their policy's actual provisions or the conditions under which the coverage is completely inapplicable. Directors are especially vulnerable after hostile takeovers when coverage is likely to change. Whatever the circumstances, the CEO should never be in the position of having neglected to point up both the *risks* and the *protective measures* taken by management in behalf of the directorate.

10. THOU SHALT, ABOVE ALL, REMAIN HUMBLE. As Yogi Berra is alleged to have said, "It's *deja vu* all over again." No CEO achieved his lofty level of seniority without not only learning the virtue of humility but also practicing it faithfully over a long period of time. It is axiomatic in almost any discipline—business, politics, sports, and especially in interpersonal relationships—when you stop doing whatever you did to get where you are, you will not stay there very long. But whatever traits and/or skills your progression to the top will require, *remaining humble* is certain to be included and—accordingly—should be jealously guarded and enhanced whenever possible.

NEVER MIND THE "BUILDUP"

Full and faithful obedience of all ten of these commandments will be no easier than for the Biblical ones, but the mere understanding of their magnitude will enhance the CEO's performance materially. It is Commandment 2 that may be the most elusive of all, not because it is vague or complex, but because it is *rarely carried out effectively*.

Why?

The key word is RECOMMEND. Such a simple word with clear-cut meaning, but so often poorly implemented. Let's consider again Commandment 2: THOU SHALT *RECOMMEND* AND CAUSE THE ESTABLISHMENT OF BASIC POLICY.

Most management recommendations are simple enough, but for some inexplicable reason they frequently get lost in the overburden of lengthy rhetoric and memoranda. This is especially so when there are new risks or "old baggage" associated with the proposal. In such cases, it is almost as though the last thing management wants to do is to be clear about the final proposal. Elaborate detail is substituted for a bold, factual conclusion, and nothing is more disconcerting or annoying to a director. Who among us, after all, wishes to be the victim of a loquacious or circuitous buildup when our vote of approval is the obvious and only purpose of it all.

SO PLEASE. Never mind the "buildup." It will almost always prove to be counterproductive. Yet I know of no other more prevalent failing of otherwise seasoned executives. It is so unnecessary and so limiting.

DIRECTORS DESERVE THE "DIRECT" APPROACH

COMMUNICATIONS—our key word at the outset of this chapter—is tough enough at best. Remember the words of Sir Winston Churchill, who said of England and America: "Two great powers separated only by a common language."[2]

Humorist and prolific author, Robert Orben, relates the return home of a college freshman for the weekend.[3] Dad asked, "How are things going?"

He said, "Good."
"How's the food?"

---

[2] Winston S. Churchill, *The Grand Alliance* (Boston: Houghton Mifflin Company, 1950), p. vi.

[3] Robert Orben, *2100 Laughs for All Occasions* (Garden City, N.Y.: Doubleday & Company, Inc., 1983), p. 42.

Directors Deserve the "Direct" Approach

He said, "Good."
"And the dormitory?"
He said, "Good."
"They've always had a strong football team. How do you think they'll do this year?"
He said, "Good."
"And how are your studies going?"
He said, "Good."
"Have you decided on your major yet?"
He said, "COMMUNICATIONS."

Not very communicative you say?
To be sure.
Yet if I have learned nothing more in my 40 years in business—26 of them spent as a CEO—BREVITY IS SECOND ONLY TO SUBSTANCE IN BOARD COMMUNICATIONS. No need for terseness. Just make it *concise and direct,* especially when you are seeking a simple expression of approval. A well-worn but effective form of memorandum would look like this:

TO: EACH DIRECTOR
FROM: (your name)
SUBJECT: (only 2 or 3 words here)
DATE: (today)

I. PROPOSAL

IT IS HEREBY RECOMMENDED THAT . . . this should be a succinct *sentence*—perhaps all caps for emphasis—summary of the proposition to be voted upon.

II. REASONS FOR THE PROPOSAL

1. In approximate order of significance . . . just go ahead here and state the case for your recommendation
2. with due consideration for the negatives or downside consequences . . . as well as recognition of
3. alternative courses of action which you believe to be inferior.

III. CONCLUSION

If it is credible to do so, perhaps relate the proposal here to the natural progression and fulfillment of the "master plan. . . ." Be sure to indicate any preliminary levels of approval the proposal has already received . . . and, of course, any long-term benefits not covered in Part II of the memo.

There is nothing profound about this approach. Yet after years of working with it effectively, I still see senior executives *burying*—literally hiding—their recommendation at the end of an overly long monograph, which sometimes does more to conceal than to reveal the logic of the proposed proposition.

Somehow, the temptation to *bury* a recommendation to directors beneath endless jargon seems to grow with the *magnitude of the project*. It is only human nature, I suppose, for a conscientious executive to want to *document the details*—indeed, to demonstrate to his superiors each of the prudent steps taken to arrive at the proposal. After all, if something should go wrong, let the record show how exhausting the research had been. Yet, any CEO with only a couple of years under his or her belt knows all too well the folly of trying to get out of the boardroom with anything close to a strong, cohesive, businesslike decision when the base document is an inch or two thick. The very length of the proposal itself—however studious and rational it may be—can appear so foreboding that not even one director will feel right about it for hours or perhaps even days or weeks. The competitive pace of most businesses simply will not tolerate such *luxurious clumsiness*.

Three instances come to mind during the author's tenure as a CEO. Each was a momentous decision involving relatively large resources, with much at stake in the final outcome, but each was activated and propelled forward with a cover-memo—precisely as outlined earlier, of no more than two pages:

- The 1963 consolidation of Texas National Bank & Trust Co. of Houston with National Bank of Commerce of Houston, to form what is now Texas Commerce Bancshares, Inc.
- The 1969 decision to construct Oklahoma City's Liberty Tower, 36-story home of what is now Oklahoma's largest financial institution, Banks of Mid-America
- The 1983 consolidation of Liberty National Bank & Trust Co. of Oklahoma City and First National Bank & Trust Co. of Tulsa

As you might expect, in each case, there were *attachments* to each cover-memo consisting of legal opinions, appraisals, financial history, pro forma statements, and a myriad of other related data, but most of these were evanescent when final words were chosen for the document proposing action by the directors.

OWNERSHIP MYOPIA

No recitation of typical shareholder traits would be complete without a *word of caution* concerning an exceedingly common one. Let's call it *ownership myopia*. Here's the Webster definition of *myopia:* "1: defective vision of distant objects; 2: deficiency of foresight."[4] It is, indeed, both a common and quite unfortunate characteristic of too many owners of businesses, especially some large owners and almost always founding owners.

To be sure, logic would hold that shareholders *should* be entitled to maintain their pro rata ownership when new capital is needed. It is, in fact, still the law in a few states that corporate owners must be given first option to purchase new stock in an amount proportionate to existing holdings, that is, their *preemptive right,* although such a privilege is no longer automatically conferred in Delaware nor in the large majority of other states.

In any case, incalculable damage can be done to a business when contrary owners are able to thwart the acquisition of new capital funds that would result in a diminution of their pro rata ownership, but that would literally catapult the business years ahead in financial strength. The motivation of such owners can range all the way from a genuine belief that new funds are unnecessary to a reluctance to invest more of their own funds in order to maintain ownership status quo.

While generalizations are hazardous, it has been the author's observation over the years that few successful businesses can fail to benefit from the periodic injection of capital and that, to miss the opportunity merely because existing owners are focusing solely on their own voting power, is an unfortunate form of *ownership myopia*.

In my early days on a commercial loan desk, when it was obvious that an overly ambitious credit applicant needed *capital instead of debt,* I used to say, "It's 10 times better to own 10 percent

---

[4] *Webster's New Collegiate Dictionary* (Springfield, Mass.; G. & C. Merriam Co., 1979), p. 755.

of a $10 million dollar business than 100 percent of a $100,000 business!" While it often fell on deaf ears, I was occasionally later rewarded "tenfold" by a warm word of gratitude for having *opened the eyes* of heavy borrowers to the long-range benefits of giving up ownership instead of incurring more debt.

CLOSE ENOUGH TO BE SUPPORTIVE—DISTANT ENOUGH TO BE OBJECTIVE

A board of directors that never renews itself, both with additions and retirements, risks either becoming a *captive* of management or a source of *obstruction*.

While there is no single criterion for board candidacy, a precise screening process is imperative for any well-run corporation. Fortunately, there are numerous sources of assistance on this subject, but the key is to achieve a consistently steady flow of "new blood" on the board. But new additions to the board will soon perceive their roles to be a mere sham if there is no clear-cut *board retirement policy* applicable uniformly to those who preceded them—without regard for tenure; except, of course, large ownerships are entitled to some form of representational continuity. Nothing can be more debilitating to professional management or a conscientious set of directors, however, than needless exceptions to this immutable fact of corporate life.

A SOPHISTICATED INVESTOR IS ONE WHO HAS LOST MONEY

A long-time personal friend—a CEO of more than 30 years—could not resist not long ago giving the analysts a little dig: "When we were having our troubles a few years ago, all of Wall Street took notice, and our stock price dropped like a rock. When things got better, both in terms of reporting good interim results and favorable future prospects, our price/earnings ratio didn't move an inch! What I want to know," he almost shouted, "is where are all those (bleep, bleep) Wall Street rocket scientists and Rhodes Scholars when we need them most?"

One would think that seasoned investors (or their analysts) would be fair in both directions as a company's earning power ebbs and flows. But sadly, it just does not work that way. Once burned, the investor achieves a degree of pseudo-sophistication that is kin to deafness and only a three- to five-year period of exemplary performance can begin to restore their following.

So we will close this chapter with the admonition that understanding shareholder relationships means—as a minimum—*understanding how unforgiving they can be* and how vital it is to keep *all* their lines of communication open.

But that is how this chapter began. Are there no more specific guidelines than that? Yes, for your consideration, there are a few more proven ones:

- Maintain an effective *month-to-month contact program* with the investment community, especially with institutions that represent large ownership.
- Cultivate *greater research coverage* by several organized Wall Street and regional firms.
- Commit to a limited schedule of meetings with institutional investors in major U.S. cities and perhaps abroad.
- Make the annual report your personal hobby both as to *content and format*.
- Be sure that all shareholder inquiries receive a *personal* response.
- Push for wider acceptance of *dividend reinvestment and employee stock purchase plans.*
- Work steadily to *improve your communications skills;* talk, do not read to your directors, shareholders, and staff.
- At all times, *protect your credibility by being candid;* insincerity has a quickly recognized scent, and it is not a fragrance.

If you fear the "arrogant analysts," just reflect for a moment on the dozens of testimonials the most abrasive of them have given over the years to chief executives who have been the first to admit mistakes, patiently answer what they could, find out and report back the rest, and generally drop all pretense in behalf of good, solid COMMUNICATIONS with the financial media.

Above all, *avoid whining* about the economy or other uncontrollable elements. Remember the words of Peter Drucker: "Executives are evaluated on the basis of the results they achieve, not the difficulties they encounter."[5]

One of the basic difficulties inevitably encountered by the CEO is the dreaded unfavorable turn in the economy. Understanding and coping with such events is imperative and, therefore, the subject of the next chapter.

---

[5] Peter Drucker, *The Practice of Management* (New York, Harper & Row, 1954), p. 130.

Chapter 7

UNDERSTANDING TRENDS AND CYCLES

Join any group but the consensus.
—Anonymous

NO LONGER A HO-HUM SUBJECT

Movement in the basic underlying forces that shape the economic environment in which we live and work used to be thought of as merely a dull, esoteric subject reserved essentially for specialists in the field. Unprecedented volatility has changed all this.

Few if any businesses or chief executives have been unaffected by the sharp fluctuations in business conditions, the rate of inflation, and attendant movement in interest rates of recent years. Yet some are saying that reliable techniques for recognizing and anticipating trends and cycles are more elusive than ever. In his book, entitled *Business Without Economists,* William J. Hudson even boldly claims that "business leaders routinely make more reliable forecasts than paid economists do."[1] Because the predictions of economists are so notoriously inaccurate, he goes on to

---
[1] William J. Hudson, *Business without Economists* (New York: AMACOM, 1987), p. 1.

suggest that business leaders should consider whether they can conduct their affairs more profitably without economists. His "conclusion" proclaims that "No individual forecaster, much less a consensus, will ever predict the surprises on which the real world turns."[2] He contends, "The consensus did not predict OPEC, nor the demise of OPEC. The consensus did not predict Volker's tight money policy, nor its release. The consensus did not predict the Reagan GNP boom, nor its stagnation."

Although economics is not a science of the same order as chemistry or physics, it has never claimed to be. My own view is that it would be a gross error for business men and women to ignore all economists henceforth in favor of their own individual hunches. As someone has said, "An economist is like a hunting dog. Be sure to take him on the hunt—but just don't give him the gun."

In any case, the premium on the executive's ability—FIRST, to recognize and identify economic trends by type (secular, cyclical, seasonal, and random), and SECOND, to react effectively to them—has never been greater. And hunches should not be ruled out either.

IS YOUR CEO VISION 20/20?

In his recently published book, T. Boone Pickens, Jr., comments rather succinctly on management vision:

> There are three kinds of management. Some see changes coming well in advance and may even accelerate the process. Some see changes coming just in time to adjust before it's too late. Some never see changes coming, so they don't adjust. The last group gets run over by change and it almost always comprises the arrogant, iron-headed managements who have had it their way for years and, by God, they are going to keep it their way. Good-bye to management that can't adjust.[3]

In ophthalmological terms, 20/20 is said to be normal vision. Also, 20/40 vision would apply to a patient who sees with the same

[2] Ibid., p. 152.

[3] Excerpted from BOONE, by T. Boone Pickens, Jr. Copyright 1987 T. Boone Pickens, Jr. and Beatrice Carr Pickens. Reprinted by permission of Houghton Mifflin Company and Lescher & Lescher, Ltd.

clarity at 20 feet what someone with normal vision sees at 40 feet; likewise 20/80 vision would mean the patient's vision was so poor that his or her vision at 20 feet was no better than normal vision at 80 feet; and 20/200 vision is said to be legal blindness.

How interesting it would be if CEOs could be tested for their economic vision: their individual ability to see the real dynamics, the basic things going on that effectively determine the course of business conditions. Regrettably this is not a very practical idea, although in time such an approach might very well emerge, at least experimentally.

Meanwhile it would be well, I'm sure, for business executives—and, for that matter, everyone else—to guard against becoming victims of *hyperopia* (another proprietary term of ophthalmologists—forgive me) meaning, in a word, farsightedness; a preoccupation with the so-called big picture and little or no concern for the day-to-day chores that surround us. It is the latter that can become so troublesome that one's perception of the big picture becomes quite incidental.

HOW LONG IS "LONG TERM"?

Hyperopia does, of course, have its place and indeed is invaluable in the recognition of *secular trends* referred to earlier. One dictionary definition of "secular" is: "long-term, coming once in an age." Familiar examples of such blockbuster trends would include:

- The explosive expansion of air travel[4], with its enormous social and economic ramifications
- Instantaneous satellite communication, with its incredible impact on our lives generally, and especially the way in which it revolutionized financial markets
- The rapid advancement of medical science, with its dramatic effect on life expectancy—already twice what it was 200 years ago
- The economic emancipation of women, with its bold attendant changes in our so-called styles of life

[4] General Dynamics, McDonnell Douglas, and Rockwell International each were recently awarded $25 million contracts to design the X-30, a hypersonic plane envisioned to fly between New York and Tokyo in two hours.

- The steady growth of massive foreign productivity, with all its competitive implications and threats to the nation's economy.

By the year 2000, who would dare say where these secular trends will have led, or what new ones will emerge to shape our complex world in the new century? If you feel that such a formidable question is *not* for you, then perhaps *neither is the role of chief executive*. Whether you are accurate or not in your perception of long-term trends, the owners of almost any business—as well as those who follow you in its employ—are entitled to know that its leader is at least committed to try. After all, the world is now spending about $1 billion every business day on scientific research.

How does one begin to sense the emergence of major *secular trends?* Here are just a couple of clues to possible developments that could indeed have indelible *secular* effects on every business enterprise, large and small:

A WORLDWIDE ENERGY SYSTEM

- Electric power is so pervasive in our lives that we take it for granted until there is a power failure.
- Connecting existing regional power grids is now well within reach technically.[5]
- With the world population already at 5 billion, inadequate electric power could lead to a wide range of chaotic conditions.
- It has been estimated that the cost of one mile of ultra-high voltage is about $1 million or $25 billion to circle the earth—only 5 percent of the combined annual U.S./USSR military budgets.[6]
- Finally, nothing could affect lagging standards of living more quickly or more permanently than *one world of electricity*.

---

[5] R. Buckminster Fuller, *A Worldwide Energy System* (San Diego, Global Energy Network, International, 1987), executive summary, pp. 1–5. Courtesy Buckminster Fuller Institute, Los Angeles.

[6] Ibid.

CNG FUELS[7]

- Compressed Natural Gas (CNG) is now the official fuel for the official car for Governor Henry Bellmon of Oklahoma. Within a two-year period, 100 state and municipal vehicles will have natural gas fuel capabilities.
- "Natural gas is cleaner, safer, and more efficient than gasoline," the governor said.
- Oklahoma Natural Gas Company claims that CNG can also be delivered to fleet users at a cost savings of about 37 cents for each equivalent gallon.
- The worldwide effect of such a drastic change on both *air quality* and the *cost of ground transportation* could be enormous.

By the same token, few things can have more effect on the performance of the chief executive than the capacity to read the secular "tea leaves" and assess the economic environment in which a business will find itself over the longer term.

In hindsight, whenever surveys are conducted to identify leading business executives, almost without fail such an ability is a primary criterion. Of John S. Reed, chairman and CEO of Citicorp, it was said by one observer, "He's thinking ahead 10 to 15 years. He has an amazing gift for seeing what's going to happen."[8] Others in the same poll were also cited for "vision and foresight." But *they were not born with such talent,* and that should encourage the rest of us to follow their example.

HOW LONG IS A "CYCLE"?

For centuries, scholars throughout the world have proclaimed the existence of cycles in human behavior and, more particularly, as recorded by economic data. While few contend that periods of

---

[7] *Flame Tips,* vol. 18, no. 5, Oklahoma Natural Gas Company, Tulsa (January 1978).

[8] William E. Gould, "America's Best CEOs," *Industry Week* (August 10, 1987), p. 37.

prosperity and depression do not alternate over time, there is little agreement as to the normal length of time required for the process to occur.

As early as 1926, N.D. Kondratieff did the first empirical work to establish the case for the existence of very long waves in the world economy with cycles requiring 25 to 30 years to repeat themselves (if not interrupted first by war).[9] More recently, Indian scholars have documented decade-long swings, and one of their followers claims that the United States, after experiencing 7 years of prosperity from 1983 through 1989, will suffer 7 years of economic depression from 1990 through 1996 with a stock market plunge likely coming toward the end of 1989, or, at the latest, the first quarter of 1990.[10]

Former economic counsel to Presidents Kennedy, Johnson, and Nixon, Pierre A. Rinfret, leads a host of other economists who are highly skeptical of such "mumbo jumbo," meaning not that cyclical economics is a myth but rather that there is no precise interval of time between phases which can be relied upon.[11] A leading exponent of this same point of view, Dr. Arthur B. Adams, a former dean of business at the University of Oklahoma, advanced his own thesis more than 50 years ago which to this day stands as a landmark work concerning the nature of cyclical fluctuation in business conditions.[12]

Adams was much more interested in the characteristics and interrelationships of the different phases of cyclical movements, what causes them, and what reforms might eliminate their extremes than he was in discovering precisely how often they occur. Indeed, his overriding conclusion (in my language, not his) was that WE ARE NOT DOOMED BY ECONOMIC CIRCUMSTANCE. While his data clearly identified four distinct phases—BOOM, LIQUIDATION (today we say "recession"), DEPRESSION, and RE-

[9] N. D. Kondratieff, "The Long Waves of Economic Life," *Review of Economic Statistics* (1935), p. 14.

[10] Ravi Batra, economics professor at Southern Methodist University, rev. by Stephen J. Govoni," "Transcendental Trepidation," *Financial World* (July 28, 1987), p. 24.

[11] Ibid., p. 25.

[12] Arthur B. Adams, *Analysis of Business Cycles* (New York: McGraw Hill, 1936).

COVERY—he found no reliable evidence that there is a causal relationship between them. He flatly denied that "The first phase of any cycle is generated or caused by forces or conditions which developed during the last phase of the cycle which preceded it."[13] And nowhere in his writing can one find the slightest suggestion that cyclical phenomena recur within a reliably repeating interval of time.

How long is a "cycle"?

Dean Adams, I believe, would hold that the duration of a given cycle would be dependent on an almost infinite number of variables. In fact, he did say, "There have been many periods of time in our industrial and business history when our economic system was not passing through any perceptible period of a business cycle."[14]

This rather matter-of-fact condition must be disappointing to those who fail to realize that it is gross oversimplification to think that the trend will always be clearly up or down. Horizontal movement of long duration may be dull, but it is much more acceptable than downward—and it does, nevertheless, happen to be the real world as we have known it thus far.

HOW LONG IS "SEASONAL"?

The dictionary definition of seasonal I like best is "the time when something specified flourishes, develops, takes place, is popular, permitted, or is at its best."[15] I like this best because it recognizes that seasonal trends may transcend the four quarterly calendar seasons of the year. In other words, as a chief executive officer you must realize that you may perceive some condition in your business to be "seasonal" (that is, less than cyclical in its likely duration) but which may well endure longer than the actual spring, summer, fall, or winter of a given year. It may remain "popular" or be "permitted" by a relaxed law or regulatory ruling, but not be in any way

---

[13] Ibid., p. 42.
[14] Ibid., p. 44.
[15] *Webster's New World Dictionary,* 2nd college ed. (New York: The World Publishing Company, 1972), p. 1285.

comparable in its impact to a cyclical trend. Yet it should not be ignored.

The boomerang, hula hoop, pogo stick, and paddle tennis all enjoyed their "season"—each longer than 12 months. But they were "trendy" items that faded as rapidly as they were spawned. Erma Bombeck writes about others: a Japanese fiber-optic wedding gown that glows in the dark, an automatic bread maker that kneads the dough as you sleep; an electronic bridge score pad, and a portable instrument that tells you where the sweet spot is on your golf ball. "All flukes," she said, meaning their "season" was brief—indeed, some were even shorter than the spring, summer, fall, or winter of a given year.

And so it is in most businesses. The executive should be aware of such temporal trends which (for lack of better terminology) we call "seasonal" and which may be gone before we can adjust to them.

HOW LONG IS "RANDOM"?

The dictionary definition of random I like best is "that which seemingly happens by chance or is done, made or said without regard for its consequences."[16] I like this best because it recognizes that random trends (or events) can only be anticipated by chance. In other words, as chief executive officer you should not be held accountable for such events. Fortunately most such contingencies can be insured against, that is, earthquakes, floods, even mud slides (except in certain areas).

Regrettably, however, some can neither be anticipated or insured against. A staggering recent example in our part of the world was the sudden demise of OPEC, which witnessed a decline of nearly 70 percent in energy prices (from high to low) in only a year's time. While cheaper energy was a welcome event for consumers, its suddenness caused costly dislocation of an industry very much at the core of our national security. Even more tragic was that some CEOs were held accountable for this random event by both regulators and owners of financial institutions. In any case, random change can be anticipated only by a clairvoyant.

[16] Ibid., p. 1176.

HOW TO COPE?

This chapter's declared purpose was to contribute to the reader's understanding of "trends and cycles" and especially the value of perceiving the direction of all but the random ones in advance. Yet Ranier Maria Rilke makes such an effort seem so fruitless with this observation, "Nothing in this world can one imagine beforehand, not the least thing; everything is made up of so many unique particulars that it cannot be foreseen."[17] My own view, however, is closer to that of the renowned Charles Schwab, who said, "Keeping a little ahead of conditions is one of the secrets of business; the trailer seldom goes far."[18]

How best, then, to make the effort? How to cope with a task which some say simply cannot be done, yet which others contend must be done—at least, "a little"?

The author will not pretend to possess a charmed formula for staying a little ahead of conditions at all times, but it is possible to mention *two proven qualities* that will serve you well in your own individual effort and under your own unique circumstances.

The FIRST of the two qualities needed to tip the scales in your favor is simply the NEED TO BE MORE OBSERVANT. If you already feel you are, take a minute (exactly 60 seconds), if you will, and accept the challenge of some very talented management consultants[19] to *count the number of letters "f"* in the following sentence:

> FINISHED FILES ARE THE RESULT OF YEARS OF SCIENTIFIC STUDY COMBINED WITH THE EXPERIENCE OF MANY YEARS.

Time's up. Tell me honestly, now, did you count 3 or more? 4 or more? 5 or more? 6 or more? or 7 or more?

Careful.

---

[17] Ranier Maria Rilke, "Thoughts on the Business of Life," *Forbes,* October 19, 1987, p. 224.

[18] Charles Schwab, Ibid., p. 224.

[19] New Age Thinking Pacific Institute, Inc., Seattle.

There are *only* 6 "f"s.

If you counted fewer than 6, I am certain your powers of observation will improve quickly, and that, in turn, should persuade you that your daily powers of observation on the job just might be strengthened as well. Trust me.

The SECOND of the two qualities needed and which I can certainly attest should also improve your perception of business trends is the NEED TO BE MORE INDEPENDENT. If you already feel you are, take a moment please and just think slowly about the timeless words of California's former senior senator, S.I. Hayakawa:

> "If you see
> in any given situation only
> what everybody else can see,
> you can be said to be
> so much a representative
> of your culture
> that you may be a victim to it."

Tell me. Can you honestly say that you need *not* improve your *independence?* . . . especially in your reading of the daily news? . . . especially in your acceptance or rejection of the claims of politicians during elections? . . . and especially in your absorption of the economic data concerning trends and cycles that come to your attention?

My feeling is that once you have put these two great needs in place:

the need to be more observant
and
the need to be more independent;
it is then that you will also become:
more objective;
and when you become more *observant,* more *independent,*
and more *objective,* you are also about to become:
more creative;
and when you become more *observant,* more *independent,*

more *objective* and more *creative,*
you are finally also about to become:
more *productive.*

AND THAT, PATIENT READER, WILL ALMOST SURELY MAKE YOU A SUPERIOR CHIEF EXECUTIVE. Again, trust me. At the very least you will be much better able *to recognize and cope with trends and cycles.*

LAISSEZ FAIRE—ALWAYS? SOMETIMES? NEVER?

Webster defines laissez faire as "the policy of letting the owners of industry and business fix the rules of competition, conditions of labor, and so forth, as they please without governmental regulation or control." Or, in a word, "*non-interference.*" In the history of almost every free nation in the world, the ebb and flow of "non-interference" policies can be traced with uncanny accuracy merely by plotting profitability trends of business that serve the masses.

Both the "overkill" of regulation and "hands off" by the regulators can bring an industry to its knees. A prime example of the former in the United States, of course, would be the railroads, while the airlines sadly have succumbed to the latter.

Then came banking with the shocking evaporation of its long entrenched profit margin when Regulation Q—the one which prohibited payment of interest on demand deposits—was allowed to expire on April 1, 1986.[20] There always is some pseudomarketing maverick who decides to "be the leader" in paying the top interest rate and temporarily (he thinks) sacrifices earnings in behalf of demand deposit market share. You know the rest. Every other wide-awake bank in the market is compelled to follow or sacrifice market share—and the traditional margin is history. Why? Because if anyone dares to attempt a return to lower rates paid, he is automatically stalled out of the game.

What a shame that—seemingly—we need some regulation just to protect us from our greedy and irresponsible selves. To be sure, a

---

[20] The Federal Reserve System, through its so-called Regulation Q, had previously restricted the payment of interest on the deposits of its member banks.

healthy and profitable banking system really is in the public's best interest. But should it be subsidized by arbitrary and protective regulation?

As a banker for 40 years, the author finds the notion totally repugnant. Yet, the author also knows very well how futile it would be to expect corporate executives in any industry not to indulge in "cutthroat" competition in the short run, even at the cost of significant diminution in earnings.

Whoever said, "When you are served a lemon, make lemonade!" must have had deregulation in mind. Frankly I'm not really concerned—long term—as to how creative bank management will cope with the consequences of deregulation. "Lemonade" is already being mentally brewed in the form of other services and expansion across geographic boundaries when the removal of the Glass Steagall Act and interstate banking hurdles has finally occurred.

Meanwhile, until the trend is complete, I must say it's mighty tempting to say simply, LAISSEZ FAIRE—MORE OFTEN THAN NOT, BUT NOT ALWAYS.

NOT TO WORRY

One final word concerning trends, especially when none of these suggestions are particularly helpful and you misread them with negative consequences: IF YOU WALLOW IN THE NEGATIVES, YOU WILL NOT BE READY—OR PERHAPS EVEN RECOGNIZE—THE POSITIVES WHEN THEY COME ALONG.

Perhaps you will remember the ancient rhyme of a nameless 15-year-old boy who, growing tired of his grandfather's pessimism, wrote the following:

> My granddad, viewing Earth's worn cogs,
> Said things were going to the dogs;
> His granddad, in his house of logs,
> Said things were going to the dogs;
> His granddad, in the Flemish bogs,
> Said things were going to the dogs;

His granddad, in his old skin togs,
Said things were going to the dogs;
There's one thing I have to state—
The dogs have had a good long wait!

In other words, do not be discouraged if your ability to sense future trends and cycles in advance yields a spotty record. You will not be alone. And such failures need not cause you to give the challenge an undue commitment of your future time and energy. Indeed, the next chapter concerning the broader duties of "the boss" also deserves its "pound of flesh" and can literally consume you.

Chapter 8

UNDERSTANDING THE CEO'S BROADER OBLIGATIONS

If we got paid for doing some of the things we do—we wouldn't do them.
—Anonymous

DANIEL WEBSTER NAILED IT

In case you are in any doubt concerning a chief executive's *broader duties* beyond his business regimen and personal commitments, we need search no further than the epic words of the eloquent Daniel Webster: "Let our object be our country, our whole country, and nothing but our country."[1] Surely when he used the word "country," he meant to include volunteer community and civic work too. What a different country we would have without these. Whether he meant that or not, let me assure you that, as a CEO, *your fate as a community servant is sealed,* so why not enjoy it? Indeed, why not assert yourself and volunteer for something you can enjoy? After all, we really are obliged to pay "civic rent" for the space we occupy, aren't we?

---

[1] Daniel Webster, *Useful Quotations* (New York: Grosset & Dunlap, 1933), p. 104.

THINK "EXTRACURRICULAR"

On some campuses, extra credit is awarded for certain extracurricular activities. While the CEO does not enjoy such a perquisite, she nevertheless may well be evaluated in the minds of many constituents—albeit more subtly—for her involvement in community affairs, especially so if there is a sociological or humanitarian dimension. Obviously, such activity can be overdone to the detriment of both the individual, the family, and her business. But, for it to be done well, the busy CEO will need to make community involvement a consciously high priority.

A "GUT DECISION"

One's so-called "peace of mind" concerning the expenditure of his or her time and energy runs well beyond "extracurricular activity." An unforgettable incident comes to mind in which a now prominent national figure made an abrupt career change based entirely on his perceived "peace of mind"—more accurately, his "calm of stomach."

The year was 1960. George Herbert Walker Bush was president and CEO of Zapata Offshore Drilling Company, a strong leader in its then exceedingly profitable industry. The author was in his second year as CEO of Houston's fourth-largest bank. We were Zapata's bank. The relationship was close and mutually profitable.

"Bill," he said one day, "things are going real well in the business, but it's just not for me."

I was stunned. "How on earth can you say that, George. Zapata is a role model for offshore drilling. The future is bright. Why wouldn't you be completely reassured of a strong and rewarding future?" (or words to that effect).

"It's really quite simple," he replied, and then proceeded to describe how each day he felt less and less comfortable in the pit of his stomach about his career commitment. He was not an ulcer victim, but he reasoned that it was only a matter of time.

"What sort of work would appeal to you more," I finally asked.

He did not hesitate. He looked me squarely in the eye and said, "Bill, I've decided to run for office."

For the next half hour I attempted (in vain) to change his mind. "How in the world could *politics* be easier on one's digestive system? . . . How can a Republican make it in Texas?" And on I went. I simply could not believe it. I knew I was doing the right thing in my old friend's best interest. But all I was really doing was expressing my own temperament, not his.

As I look back, I see that he was exceedingly patient, and my entreaty was wasted. And, how wrong I was. The rest makes role model history in both the Republican Party and in the annals of our nation's history of leading statesmen.

There are two addenda: 1) There were no more stomach symptoms, but 2) whenever I see him he good-naturedly admits that there are times he wishes he *had taken my advice!*

Just like our propensity for those extracurricular activities we enjoy most, career decisions also seem to work out best when we are uninhibited by duties we fundamentally do not enjoy even when they are otherwise rewarding. Finally, there's a reliable corollary here: if you can't do what you enjoy, *learn to enjoy what you do, until you can change it.*

THE SOCIOLOGICAL DIMENSION

Extracurricular activities on the sociological side run a wide gamut. One is not involved very long in business without having opportunities to become well immersed in all manner of artistic, charitable, civic, educational, health, humanitarian, and other not-for-profit endeavors. It takes a seaworthy CEO indeed to navigate these waters without beaching one's energies on the shores of too many requests—either in the form of *leadership invitations, donation requests, or both.* It is not the author's purpose here to make the case for any one or group of such "worthy causes," only to point up both the need to be involved—you will enjoy it—and also the need to be discriminating. Three or four board or committee assignments might be quite manageable for one CEO, while one or two could well be excessive for another. The single clue that might help the discrimination process is the extent to which the proposed relationship might involve financial problems. Debt-ridden community ventures are sometimes far better off being phased out—an honorable burial, if you will—rather than being allowed to limp along sapping the energies of top executives whose talents could otherwise be put to much more productive usage.

Or, instead of deliberately avoiding involvement with such a troubled project, the busy CEO might be inspired to jump in and do the "embalming," this perhaps being a more genuine service to the community in the long run. But if this is your choice, be prepared for a surprise or two along the way in terms of the extra time required to see it through.

DON'T LET FORM DEFEAT SUBSTANCE

That long list of DON'Ts in Chapter 2, of course, can never be completed, which is another way of pointing out how fruitless it is to try for perfection as a chief executive. But here is another one that deserves special treatment and fits best here because of the real-life experience which demonstrated it.

Years ago in Tulsa, I was hyperactive in the Jaycees (two to four hours per day). The local chapter had been cited repeatedly as a model organization. We had, in fact, brought the national headquarters to our city from Chicago, and we were mighty proud!

On the local scene, the Tulsa chapter for nearly three years had devoted huge amounts of time and energetic manpower to a study of three basic forms of municipal government: (1) strong mayor, (2) council/manager, and (3) independent commissioners. At least a version of two of the three forms had been tried in nearby cities of comparable size during the previous ten-year period with only modest success. The entire city was caught up in the debate, and emotions were beginning to run fairly high. While we were more than pleased with the attention the subject had attracted, some of us (after the second year) were becoming more than a little weary and quite concerned as to how we were going to "get out of the room" and bring a livable end to such a controversial city-wide flap. It was getting serious.

It seemed that everywhere we turned for guidance—and there were some excellent examples of each form of charter around the nation—we just could not document a clear-cut superiority of any one of the three approaches. In fact, for every shining example of each, there seemed to be another tarnished with abuses. How could this be?

At a breakfast meeting in early January 1951, the answer suddenly came, and each of us on the Jaycee executive committee was chagrined by its simplicity. Several of us had developed a partiality for the council/manager charter. Two larger cities (one in the East and the other in the Midwest) had made it work with notable success. But another city in the Southwest was in the process of abandoning it because—get this—there had been fraudulent collusion between a dishonest city manager and two greed-ridden commissioners. In other words, the *form of charter had proven to be quite incidental when the wrong people were elected to office.*

There is more to the story, but it did have a livable—if not happy—ending. We closed the project with two conclusions: (1) No form of city government can serve its constituency very well in the hands of unscrupulous or inept office holders; and the corollary (2) any one of several reasonably constructed charters can function effectively in the hands of competent civic servants.

In hindsight, it was just another classic case of *form versus substance*. Everyone—I mean everyone—agreed, and we all felt good about it. Substance over form also works well in the world of business.

THE "ALLEGED GAP"

While you are making up your mind which tricky maze of the volunteer world appeals most to you, one *precaution* seems in order: BEWARE OF THE ALLEGED GAP BETWEEN BUSINESS AND THE HUMANITIES. For obvious reasons, not very much is written on this subject, but whether real or perceived it is definitely a subject worthy of consideration. This is not to suggest that volunteer business people are unwelcome or resented by professionals on the humanitarian side. Only that in some minds, there is a gap to be reckoned with, at least at the outset.

Several basic differences have been cited that tend to make the general case:
- Business people are less idealistic and, therefore, not fully committed to the broad purposes of a humanitarian group.
- Business people often demonstrate careless writing skills that only mirror an inferior quality of mind.

- Business people often speak with cliché-ridden jargon or trite phrasing (like "finalize" and "prioritize") that can only be described as intellectual laziness.
- Business people look at everything too personally and tend to have many built-in biases.
- Business people, in the main, are specialists who got where they are purely by chance and are therefore ill-equipped to perform effectively concerning the community's broader sociological and humanitarian issues.

What a shame that these "gap perceptions" exist, whether deserved or not. Even the slightest chance that we have two of the more important segments of our society not in juxtaposition is regrettable. Businessmen and humanitarian intellectuals genuinely need each other. Each has the potential for stifling and retarding the other. If education and the humanities lack the support of business, then their future is suspect. By the same token, if the latter has disdain for the former, constructive and needed changes in our economic fabric may never be made.

THE WRITTEN WORD

If you squirmed or even winced a bit a few paragraphs earlier at the mere mention of *trite and overworked expressions,* THAT IS A VERY GOOD SIGN. Perhaps this is the spark that will ignite your determination to improve your communications skills. If you thought they were important to your job, the ability to communicate effectively will be all the more visible—and therefore crucial—as you move into civic work. Business clichés are commonplace because they convey well-understood meaning. On the outside, they are pedestrian.

Author of 16 books and more than 150 articles on business correspondence, William H. Butterfield says that *the typical business letter contains 30 to 50 percent more words than needed.*[2] One of his most requested handouts at his popular seminars is a piece

---

[2] Formerly chairman of the Department of Business Communication at the University of Oklahoma and past president of the American Business Communications Association.

The Written Word

entitled, "When You Write A Letter . . . Make Every Word Count" (see figure 5 for one of its six pages). His "Letter-Analysis Check List" also is worthy of close study (see Figure 6).

WEED OUT USELESS WORDS

The following sentences contain 154 words. Try to reduce this number to 77 — a saving of 50% — simply by crossing out unnecessary words. Then compare your revised sentences with those on the lower portion of this page.

1. At this point no decision has been made, and none is expected before fall. (14 words)
2. Whenever you find that we can be helpful in any way, please do not hesitate to let us know. (19 words)
3. We wish to take this opportunity to thank you for your valued patronage throughout this past year. (17 words)
4. This cost estimate, as a matter of fact, is similar in many respects to the one prepared by our Chicago office about a year or so ago. (27 words)
5. For your information I might mention that we shall open a branch office in Springfield the early part of next year. (21 words)
6. This will acknowledge and thank you for your welcome letter of May 10, which has just come to my attention. (20 words)
7. Please accept our congratulations on the fine recognition you have received in being named "Salesman of the Year." (18 words)
8. The date of this announcement, which was originally scheduled for June 5, has now been postponed until later. (18 words)

If you have deleted 77 needless words, only 77 remain:

1. No decision is expected before fall. (6 words)
2. Whenever we can be helpful, please let us know. (9 words)
3. Thank you for your patronage this past year. (8 words)
4. This cost estimate is similar to the one prepared by our Chicago office about a year ago. (17 words)
5. We shall open a branch office in Springfield early next year. (11 words)
6. Thank you for your letter of May 10. (8 words)
7. Congratulations on being named "Salesman of the Year." (8 words)
8. This announcement, originally scheduled for June 5, has been postponed. (10 words)

Figure 5 Reprinted by permission of W. H. Butterfield, Correspondence Consultant.

LETTER-ANALYSIS CHECK LIST

Here is a quick, easy way to analyze your own letters and discover any chronic faults you may have. The next time you sign your outgoing letters, apply the following check list to a few of them.

Can you answer YES to these questions?

1. Is your letter clear and easy to read, assuring the reader's quick understanding with the minimum of effort on his part?

2. If your message is intended to induce action, does it stress the reader's interests and point out benefits to him?

3. Is the tone of your letter courteous and friendly, suggesting that you enjoyed writing it?

4. Is your message well organized, containing all the necessary facts or information without irrelevant details?

5. Does your letter show consideration for the reader by revealing a genuine desire to be helpful?

6. Is your letter neat and attractive as the result of proper layout on the sheet, clean-cut typing, and short paragraphs?

Can you answer NO to these questions?

1. Does your letter contain trite, outmoded expressions, such as contents duly noted, kindly be advised, pursuant to yours of recent date, etc.?

2. Are the words I, we, us, and our used too often, indicating too much emphasis on your own interests and point of view?

3. Does your letter contain any superfluous words that contribute nothing to the sentences in which they appear?

4. Are any of your statements vague or ambiguous, and therefore liable to confuse the reader?

5. Does your letter contain any tactless words that carry connotations unpleasant to the reader?

6. Is there anything about your message that gives it the tone or appearance of a form letter?

Figure 6 Reprinted by permission of W. H. Butterfield, Correspondence Consultant.

THE SPOKEN WORD

Beryl Pfizer recently asked, "I wonder what language truck drivers are using now that everyone else is using theirs?"[3]

In discharging one's community obligations, you will find nothing more useful than the *effective delivery of the spoken word*. Literally hundreds of books and manuals are available on public speaking. Courses of instruction also abound. It is not our purpose here to compete with these rich sources of instruction. As a practical matter, however, the author has developed SEVEN SURE SPEAKING TIPS from his own "trial and error" experience which, though not terribly profound, may at least provide confirmation of some of the right and wrong approaches to the podium:

1. DON'T ACCEPT A SPEAKING ROLE IF YOU DON'T HAVE THE TIME OR DESIRE TO PREPARE—usually the *minimum* ratio of 5 to 1.
2. A SPEECH HAS THE SAME FIRST PROBLEM AS AN AUTOMOBILE—IT HAS TO GET STARTED—I suggest the use of either a humorous or provocative opening.
3. THERE ARE THREE SAFE ASSUMPTIONS ABOUT EVERY AUDIENCE—interested first in themselves, second in people, and third (maybe) in your message.
4. FEW SPEECHES ARE REMEMBERED FOR THEIR MESSAGE ALONE—the substance must be made relevant and interesting to the individual listener.
5. IF YOUR MISSION IS TO PERSUADE, CONSIDER THE LONG-ESTABLISHED "MINI-MAX" METHOD—there is minimum risk to the "buyer" and maximum potential gain.[4]
6. YOU DON'T NEED TO BE WILLIAM JENNINGS BRYAN OR WINSTON CHURCHILL—the audience will sense you are not being yourself and will be so caught up in the charade that the distraction from your message will be total;

---

[3] Beryl Pfizer, *Forbes* (January 25, 1988), p. 136.
[4] Also mentioned in Chapter 5.

7. FEW SPEECHES ARE REMEMBERED FOR THEIR LENGTH—if you don't strike oil in 15 or 20 minutes, *stop boring!*

In his book, *You Are the Message,* communications consultant, Roger Ailes says:

> Some business speakers will do almost anything to find a way not to be interesting. There's a sense among some people in business that *style* and *substance* are mutually exclusive. The perception is that if you have *style* you must be a *lightweight.* The same logic says that if you're going to demonstrate *substance,* you've got to be *boring;* then the audience will think you're one of the really bright persons who know what they're doing. This is the old way of thinking and the successful people moving up in the workplace know it. Don't join the Brotherhood of Boredom—the dues are too high.[5]

Speaking of *style,* there is one very limiting characteristic that merits close consideration, since it is the *single most noticeable difference* between the truly accomplished speaker and all the rest, in the author's opinion. Think back, if you will, to those speakers who made an indelible impression upon you as distinguished from those who were—at best—barely informative and—at worst—dull and boring. Subject matter aside, do you recall any one thing in particular that the latter group had in common? Not an easy question to be sure. Yet, when you read the next sentence, I believe you will understand immediately the thrust of the question. IT'S THAT MONOTONOUS AND REPETITIOUS INFLECTION PATTERN most speakers tend to use, repeating the same SING-SONG TEMPO with each succeeding thought. And, sadly, this common trait is not confined to the amateurs among us; some of our most experienced public office holders are the worst practitioners. In my own recollection, I would even go so far as to say that only one speaker in ten is entirely free of this careless habit.

Break away from the crowd! Don't be a victim of a limiting style that can be consciously eliminated with a little self-awareness and self-determination. Move into the *upper ten percent* as a public speaker. Be *conversational.* Then, when you've made that transi-

---

[5] Roger Ailes with Jon Kraushar, *You Are the Message* (New York, Doubleday, 1989).

tion, perhaps you will be a candidate for weaving a little *flair and drama* into your speaking style. The difference that can make was explained nearly two thousand years ago by an anonymous Greek orator who said: "When I speak, the people say, 'how well he speaks!' But when Demosthenes speaks, the people say, 'let us march!' "[6]

THE HEARD WORD

Because most of us can think much more rapidly than the normal speech rate of 150 words per minute, our racing minds often impair our hearing. Obviously, this can be especially costly in civic work.

My friend, Bill Butterfield, claims that the typical executive spends his time 9 percent in writing, 16 percent in reading, 30 percent in talking, and an incredible 45 percent in listening. Yet so little instruction is offered on HOW TO LISTEN.

- What do you mean?
- How do you know?
- What difference does it make?

Moreover, here are some all too familiar *listening faults* which too many of us unwittingly commit too much of the time:

- the *smug daydreamer* who already knows what's coming;
- the *picky fault finder* who is so preoccupied with details that the main thrust is missed;
- the *compulsive interrupter* who injects one distraction after another; and
- the *complete phoney* who fakes listening but doesn't hear a thing.

However elementary some of these concepts concerning writing, speaking, and listening may seem, the enlightened business

---

[6] Jack R. Durland, president and CEO, Cains Coffee Co., *Thirty Years of Challenging Thoughts* (unpublished pamphlet, Oklahoma City, September 1, 1981), p. 8.

executive might well review them from time to time as a means of enhancing his or her effectiveness in the civic sector.

THE ETHICAL DIMENSION

It has been said that when you lose *wealth,* you lose nothing; when you lose *health,* you lose something; but when you lose *integrity,* you lose everything. From a long-lost source, the author remembers reading of the philosophy professor who asked his class:

> "If the hood ornament of your car was a wheel, how many wheels would the car have?"
> Almost in unison the class answered, "Five."
> "Wrong," said the professor. "Calling a hood ornament a wheel doesn't make it a wheel." *Truth is not determined by popular vote.*

A recent issue of a popular business magazine carried an interesting article entitled, "FORGET ETHICS—AND SUCCEED?"[7] Thankfully the punctuation was a question mark. But the survey on which the article was based presented some *startling findings:*

- 30.6 percent of the respondents say ethics have deteriorated in the last two years.
- About half of the respondents' companies have codes of ethics, but 37.2 percent say ethical behavior is never discussed.
- About three out of ten say their boss has asked them to act unethically.
- Seven out of ten have witnessed unethical behavior in their company. Almost a third ignored it.
- A unanimous choice as to what makes ethics go sour: AMBITION. Reasons given for such shabby results included:
    - "Management doesn't care how we meet our goals—only that we get there."
    - "When I looked around, I saw others getting promoted after cheating to make their quota."

[7] Stanley J. Modic, *Industry Week,* October 19, 1987, p. 17.

The Ethical Dimension

No chief executive is likely to escape the ethical predicament: the need to BLOW THE WHISTLE, during his tenure (of reasonable length), concerning some staff activity or behavior—and HE MUST NOT EVEN HESITATE TO DO SO!

In thinking about how such CEO decisions can have an impact on the patrons of a business, the author has compiled for your consideration:

THE CUSTOMER'S BILL OF RIGHTS

In the course of economic events involving the purchase of goods or services, the buyer/customer deserves and shall be entitled to the following rights and benefits, and they shall not be alienable:

FIRST—a customer shall not be discriminated against by reason of age, gender, financial status, infirmity, race, religion, or any other criterion either real or perceived;

SECOND—a customer shall not be deceived;

THIRD—a customer shall be heard, whether legitimate questions for information or in criticism;

FOURTH—a customer shall not be charged an exorbitant price;

FIFTH—a customer shall be entitled to fair participation in a significant reduction in the cost to produce or deliver a product or service;

SIXTH—a customer shall be entitled to reasonable quality of product or service without having to make a competitive market survey;

SEVENTH—a customer shall be entitled to reasonable notice prior to a price increase;

EIGHTH—a customer should be able to discontinue the product or service for cause at will or without cause upon reasonable notification unless otherwise bound by agreement;

NINTH—a customer shall be treated with respect and courtesy;

TENTH—a customer shall also be shown due gratitude for his or her patronage, without which there is no economic event.

If these seem too formidable or virtually impossible to perform consistently, this reminder in an ancient Scottish saying can be consoling:

"WHATEVER IS RIGHTFULLY DONE, HOWEVER HUMBLE, IS NOBLE."[8]

A STILL BROADER VIEW

Understanding a CEO's broader obligations is a mammoth subject. In discussing the sociological and ethical dimensions, no inference is intended that these are by any means all-inclusive. Indeed, as we delve into the ideal criteria for CEO succession in our next chapter, we should gain an even broader view of the full package of both internal and external duties.

---

[8] Source: Ellis Mendelssohn, tailor, Oklahoma City.

Chapter 9

UNDERSTANDING CEO SUCCESSION

He's not good enough for my job—but then neither was I at his age.
—Anonymous

A CLASSIC CASE

Walter B. Wriston[1] became 65 years of age on August 3, 1984. According to Citicorp policy, this signaled his normal retirement on September 1, 1984.

No one knows how many prior months he had devoted in part to the crucial task of determining his recommendation to the directors concerning his successor. The author does know, however, that as early as mid-June 1983 no subject held more of Walt's attention. The two of us were relaxing at Twenty-One for a nonbusiness luncheon. It was a late luncheon on a Friday, and neither of us was preoccupied with our next telephone call.

After the usual pleasantries and a few typical Wriston jabs—good natured, of course—he got right with it. I cannot recall his exact words, but there was just no question—he was genuinely

---

[1] Former chairman and CEO of Citicorp, New York City.

focused. There were three uniquely qualified candidates, and the whole world knew who they were: (alphabetically) Angermueller, Reed, and Theobold. But their unique qualities compounded Mr. Wriston's task enormously. Their respective backgrounds were quite dissimilar.

His quandary was, of course, how to compare them. I could not have been more surprised or less prepared when he said, "You know each of them. Which one would you choose?" I bought a little time. The fact was, I knew them only slightly at that time although I did know that each was loaded with INTEGRITY, the cardinal requirement to be eligible for such a calling.

For quite a while I just tried to think of the key areas in which Walt himself excelled. I suppose I instinctively did so on the theory that the ongoing success and enviable momentum of Citicorp would best be sustained in the stewardship of the one who could most nearly emulate him. Of all Wriston's superior talents, two in particular leaped to mind, and I shared them with him then and there:

- First, HIS PERSPECTIVE—the rare ability to sense trends and opportunities
- Second, HIS FEEL FOR DELEGATION—the knack of judging which decisions should or should not be given group responsibility

But I added that these were by no means my sole criteria, and I asked for a few days to send him a "scorecard" on as many as ten points altogether.

He said, "Great," and we changed the subject.

Less than a week later, "my CEO candidate scorecard" (see figure 7) was on its way with the confession that "these ten points (PERSPECTIVE and DELEGATION turned out to be numbers 2 and 4, respectively) also happened to be possible chapter titles I was considering for a book I might write someday." Indeed, the "scorecard" bears a close resemblance to this book's table of contents.

His response was immediate, and read (in part) as follows:

> Many thanks for your note of June 15. I appreciated our luncheon together and, more than that, it was good of you to take time to think about my approaching problem. Your *score sheet* is *first-class* and I am sure your book will be a best seller.

CEO CANDIDATE SCORECARD
RANKING OF CANDIDATES: (1=superior; 2=good; 3=average; 4=poor)*

                                                                                     A   B   C

I. *KNOWS SELF*
(what his natural tendencies are and how best to *use* or *compensate* for them)

II. *KNOWS PERSPECTIVE*
(how to sense trends and opportunities)

III. *KNOWS WHAT IS NEEDED*
(how to assess *resources* and *talents* as well as how to acquire and develop them)

IV. *KNOWS WHEN TO DELEGATE*
(which decisions should and should *not* be given *group* responsibility)

V. *KNOWS HOW TO GET THE BEST OUT OF OTHERS*
(which one can *preside* most effectively over the other two and help others *grow*)

VI. *KNOWS HIS COMMITMENT TO BOTTOM LINE*
(how best to achieve "maximum" *sustainable* long range earning power)

VII. *KNOWS ROLE OF BOARD AND SHAREHOLDERS*
(how to strive consistently for a more *enlightened* relationship)

VIII. *KNOWS TOTAL OBLIGATION*
(that the CEO and the organization must address *sociological, political* and *humanitarian* needs)

IX. *KNOWS SIGNIFICANCE OF SUCCESSOR DEVELOPMENT*
(often apparent from his attention to this imperative in his *current* role)

X. *KNOWS SIGNIFICANCE OF PACE*
(has demonstrated the ability to *orchestrate the efforts* of others - including self - in the most productive directions and without risking massive fatigue)

* lowest score wins—and if the final score is tied—consider asking each candidate to indicate his choice, if he himself is denied.

* lowest score wins—and if the final score is tied—consider asking each candidate to indicate his choice, if he himself is denied.

Figure 7

The rest, as they say, is history. John Reed got the job. But just for the record—while I cannot document Mr. Reed's feel for DELEGATION (criterion number 4)—he certainly has come through with some incredibly timely moves that truly demonstrate his PERSPECTIVE and "sense of trends and opportunities":

- His leadership in first recognizing Citicorp's Latin American exposure in early 1987 and increasing the loan loss reserve by $3 billion
- His alert and very successful offering of $1 billion of equity, when the market received his loan write-off decision so favorably
- His companion condominium sale of office space for nearly $500 million and the attendant restoration of 1987 earnings.

Yes, it all makes for a CLASSIC CASE in understanding chief executive succession.

ANOTHER "SCORECARD" IS MUCH LONGER

From an article by Harry Levinson in the *Harvard Business Review*, we have an even more detailed approach: 20 criteria arranged in 3 categories, as follows:

THINKING

1. *Capacity to abstract,* to conceptualize, to organize, and to integrate different data into a coherent frame of reference
2. *Tolerance for ambiguity;* can stand confusion until things become clear
3. *Intelligence;* has the capacity not only to abstract, but also to be practical
4. *Judgment;* knows when to act

FEELINGS AND INTERRELATIONSHIPS

5. *Authority;* has the feeling that he or she belongs in boss's role
6. *Activity;* takes a vigorous orientation to problems and needs of the organization

7. *Achievement;* oriented toward organization's success rather than personal aggrandizement
8. *Sensitivity;* able to perceive subtleties of others' feelings
9. *Involvement;* sees oneself as a participating member of an organization
10. *Maturity;* has good relationships with authority figures
11. *Interdependence;* accepts appropriate dependency needs of others as well as of him or herself
12. *Articulateness;* makes a good impression
13. *Stamina;* has physical as well as mental energy
14. *Adaptability;* manages stress well
15. *Sense of humor;* doesn't take self too seriously

OUTWARD BEHAVIOR CHARACTERISTICS

16. *Vision;* is clear about progression of his or her own life and career, as well as where the organization should go
17. *Perseverance;* able to stick to a task and see it through regardless of the difficulties encountered
18. *Personal organization;* has a good sense of time
19. *Integrity;* has a well-established value system, which has been tested in various ways in the past
20. *Social responsibility;* appreciates the need to assume leadership with respect to that responsibility[2]

TO "SEARCH" OR "NOT TO SEARCH"?

One of the most controversial questions known to the world of business is whether CEO succession should occur from "within" or "without." The quandary is heightened by the fact that there are highly successful precedents for each of these alternatives, as well as embarrassing failures. The engagement of a search consultant—more commonly called a "head hunter"—is possible under either

---

[2] Reprinted by permission of the *Harvard Business Review* from an exhibit in "Criteria for Choosing Chief Executives" by Harry Levinson. *Harvard Business Review*, July–August, 1980, pp. 114–116. Copyright © 1980 by the President and Fellows of Harvard College; all rights reserved.

approach, but more often when the decision is made to "go outside."

The obvious benefits of engaging a search firm include:

- An independent and, hopefully, more objective assessment of the eligible candidates
- A theoretically greater chance of finding eligible candidates
- Less chance for company politics to be involved

But there are disadvantages:

- The implication that no one in the organization was sufficiently capable to move up
- The risk of too long a search process affecting operations
- The increased danger of key resignations, particularly if an outsider is chosen

The single truth, on which there is little debate, however, is that FROM THE DAY YOU GET THE CEO MANTLE, YOU SHOULD UNDERSTAND HOW ESSENTIAL IT IS FOR YOU TO GROOM *TWO OR MORE ACCEPTABLE CANDIDATES* TO SUCCEED YOU, WELL IN ADVANCE OF YOUR NORMAL RETIREMENT (OR PREPLANNED DECISION TO MOVE ON). The imperative of early development of alternative candidates for succession by the CEO simply cannot be overstated. Besides, business historians are rarely kind to those who—for any reason—fail to do so. Oh yes, please be aware that even when you do groom succession candidates, the owners (or their representatives on the board) may well choose to preempt the final selection process themselves—or perhaps even name other candidates.

PRINCIPAL PITFALLS TO BE AVOIDED

A candidate for the top management post in any business organization should be mindful of certain traits that have tripped numerous otherwise well-qualified individuals—especially those who have perceived themselves next in line of succession.

The "Clean Exit"—A Skill or an Art?

Errors of judgment committed by so-called "heirs apparent" include the following:

1. *Intoxicated with power*—so preoccupied with authority already achieved that one's conduct in relationships with others becomes insufferable.
2. *The myth of infallibility*—the supposition that one's status, in itself, insures right decisions (closely related to number 1 above).
3. *Goal gradient syndrome*[3]—defined as the tendency to become compulsively eager to reach a goal as one gets closer to it.
4. *Go-it-alone insecurity*—the need to demonstrate at all costs that one is an independent thinker.
5. *Hyper-political activist*—the important candidate who "polinates" each director with his compelling and irresistible qualities for the job.
6. *Disrespect for the incumbent*—the fatal blunder of already "counting out" the current CEO.
7. *Fox-hole mentality*—so fearful of making a mistake on the eve of the eagerly wished for promotion that nothing is ventured.

THE "CLEAN EXIT"—A SKILL OR AN ART?

There would have been a time—unquestionably—in the author's business life when making a so-called "clean exit" from the CEO's role would have been characterized here (like salesmanship) as a *skill* that can be learned rather than an art with which one must be endowed at birth. However, having observed some fairly traumatic and highly subjective failures on the part of otherwise competent executives who just could not pull it off gracefully, it may well be more an art or talent than a skill.

At the very least (having just experienced it), "passing the gavel" to a successor and, more importantly, daring not to intervene afterwards is indeed a formidable task. It may well be that some otherwise highly competent BOSSES are simply neither

---

[3] Harry Levinson, Ph.D., psychologist, and management consultant, "Heirs Apparent Often Trip," *Wall Street Journal* (March 24, 1987), p. 29.

psychologically nor emotionally equipped to do so. Whatever label fits you (if any), when it is your time to make your *exit* and make it *cleanly,* one suggestion may be useful: AT LEAST FOR A WHILE, IT'S O.K. TO "FLUNK" RETIREMENT (meaning: *stay busy!*).

You must find other productive or creative interests—*and be quick about it*—if you are to resist the enormous temptation to meddle with what will almost always seem to be the inept performance of your successor. Besides, who among us wants to make "A" in retirement?

In my own case, at my normal retirement age (65)—in order to make my exit a completely good-natured and nonthreatening one—I presented my successor with *three envelopes:*

- The *first* was to be opened "when things aren't going well" and read inside: "BLAME J. W. McLEAN."
- The *second* was to be opened "when things are really tough" and read inside: "BLAME THE DAMNED BANK EXAMINERS."
- The *third* was to be opened "when things are intolerable" and read inside: "PREPARE THREE ENVELOPES FOR YOUR SUCCESSOR!"

BRAINS: THE ULTIMATE ASSET

Back in 1983, *Fortune* magazine's survey of its "*Fortune* 500 Largest Companies" yielded the startling fact that, within a three-year period, 35 of the 100 largest were "due to change leaders."[4] Since that time, those CEO replacements have come and gone with a wide variety of types both emerging and dropping by the wayside. The types have varied from what *Fortune* calls *tightfisted bottom-line managers* to the so called *strong marketers.* There are, of course, times when each is either "in" or "out" of vogue. But what that really demonstrates is that the ones who survive are the ones *who transcend their individual tendencies and demonstrate their versatility*—remember Chapter 1—indeed, THE ONES WITH BRAINS ENOUGH TO ADJUST AND MOVE AHEAD. But:

[4] The issue of May 2, 1983.

Brains: The Ultimate Asset

- brains without *desire,*
- brains without *determination,*
- brains without *empathy,*
- brains without *humility,*
- brains without *judgment,*
- brains without *loyalty,*
- brains without *patience,* and
- brains without *faith*

will likely produce only mediocre results at best. In any case, please be aware that the only successful substitute for brains is SILENCE.

Whether a CEO candidate is a *tightfisted bottom-line manager,* a *strong marketer,* or a *versatile practitioner* or both, he would be well advised to give early consideration to the various forms of *stress* to which the "boss" is uniquely subjected—the theme of Chapter 10.

Chapter 10

UNDERSTANDING CEO STRESS

Nothing is as bad as you thought it would be—or as good.
—Anonymous

A VERY BAD JOKE

One of the classic witticisms concerning stress goes like this: "I took my doctor's advice—relaxed—*and lost my job!*" The ironic fact is that, while a relaxed state of mind is indeed the opposite of a stressful state of mind, not all forms of stress can be remedied in the same relaxed manner.

THE OTHER EXTREME

A leading Presbyterian Hospital publication cautions against the other extreme (the opposite of "relaxing") in the forms of:

TWELVE EXERCISES NOBODY NEEDS

1. *jumping* to conclusions
2. *running* around in circles
3. *wading* through paperwork
4. *pushing* your luck
5. *passing* the buck
6. *throwing* your weight around
7. *jumping* on the bandwagon
8. *spinning* your wheels
9. *dragging* your heels
10. *adding* fuel to fire
11. *climbing* the walls
12. *grasping* at straws[1]

The author's wife of more than 45 years actually found these. I could hardly blame her for feeling I have committed each of them with regularity. But for her enormous (and I fear too often thankless) support over the years, she's *entitled!*

OUR OBJECTIVE

In this chapter we will address some of the more common *forms* or levels of stress, the basic *sources* of stress that chief executives are likely to encounter, along with a selection of some of the usually effective *remedies*. Our objective will be to point up the value—both to the organization and the individual—of physical, mental, and emotional care in the all-important task of *pacing oneself*.

STRESS LEVELS

Research has shown that *some stress is acceptable* and can, in fact, be beneficial to job performance. The level of acceptability, of course, varies with the individual and the severity of the stress

---

[1] *Cardiac Club News,* vol. 6, no. 17 (June 1987).

itself—its causes and consequence. About five years ago, a university research team did some important work concerning the various levels of stress and the corresponding characteristics for bank CEOs. Their data strongly indicated five distinct stress *levels,* that may describe an executive at any point in time:

> LEVEL 0: No indication of negative stress-burnout.
>
> LEVEL 1: *Concerned about image.* Needs to be thought of as competent; likes the intensity of challenge and adventure; enjoys leadership and responsibility; and takes pride in the job and achieves more than others.
>
> LEVEL 2: *More tired lately.* Mood swings are more negative and emphasis is on the problems; irritable and impatient; feels restless and cannot concentrate.
>
> LEVEL 3: *Seriously questions worth of efforts.* Seriously considering leaving the problem-causing situation; others are not pulling their weight; constantly tired, or needs more sleep, or can't sleep.
>
> LEVEL 4: *Constantly depressed.* There is no joy and nothing to live for; you don't give a damn; you want to sleep all day; you are losing touch with reality.[2]

The West Virginia University team used a four-part questionnaire to detect which of the five stress levels best fit the respondent:

> Part 1—basic personal data, marital status, employment history, finances, and so forth
>
> Part 2—19 questions calculated to identify occupational pressures
>
> Part 3—42 questions calculated to measure the severity of the occupational stress
>
> Part 4—29 questions calculated to weigh the internal and external factors involved
>
> An elaborate process, to be sure.

---

[2] Used with permission of Professor Don P. Holdren, Ph.D., Center of Excellence in Banking, East Tennessee State University, College of Business, P. O. Box 21070A, Johnson City, Tennessee, 37614-0002.

Other studies have actually constructed a STRESS TEST, assigning point values to more than 40 so-called events (death, divorce, litigation, and so forth) that—depending on a Yes or No answer by the respondent—are then totaled.[3] A score of 150 or more—revealing a relative high level of recent stressful experiences—indicates a "50-50 chance of developing an illness or impending health change." A score in excess of 300—revealing an alarming level of recent stressful experiences—means "a 90 percent chance of an impending health change."

FINDING AN ELUSIVE REMEDY

It is this writer's (admittedly untrained) observation, however, that assessing the severity of stress—its so-called "level"—is much less elusive than the task of prescribing its remedies. It has been my observation over the years that an effective remedy for stress must be as distinctive as the stressed individual involved. Otherwise the process of relief can be endless or, at least, only temporary. *There are seemingly no standard cures and no quick fixes.* Indeed, professional help may be the truly shortest and only practical route in many cases. But if you are interested in a few basic approaches that have sometimes yielded better than average results for others, I submit the following eight for consideration:

APPROACH 1—ATTITUDE

In meeting most of life's challenges, one's attitude is crucial. As John W. Gardner said, "We are continually faced by great opportunities brilliantly disguised as insoluble problems."[4] And so it is with stress. How tempting it is to surrender to it and wallow in a sea of self-pity. Plutarch said, "The measure of a man is the way he bears up under misfortune."[5] John D. Rockefeller said, "There is no feeling in this world to be compared with self reliance—do not

---

[3] Kenneth R. Pelletier, Ph.D., *Mind as Healer Mind as Slayer* (New York: Delacorte/S. Lawrence, 1977), pp. 110–111.

[4] John W. Gardner, Ph.D., Forbes (January 16, 1984), p. 140.

[5] Ibid., p. 140.

sacrifice that to anything else." Indeed, every psychological antidote for stress begins with attitude.

APPROACH 2—HUMOR

Psychiatrists say that there is no greater catharsis than laughter at one's self. You've never really laughed at yourself until you've seen yourself sleeping. You never know what you can do until you have to undo what you did. If you can keep your head when others all about you are losing theirs, maybe you don't understand the situation.

It is perfectly O.K. to laugh at the expense of others too—but only IF it is done good naturedly, of course. Some cogent points can, in fact, be made that way, and when this happens the humorist sometimes can achieve a dual purpose: (1) She amuses and (2) she just might leave an indelible impression of a serious point on her listeners.

Last year, Democratic presidential candidate Paul Simon pulled it off beautifully. A prolific author himself, all he said in response to a request for a comment on his opponents was, "Well, why should I when the voters will learn soon enough that—collectively they have only finished one book? . . . not *writing*," he added, "*reading*."

APPROACH 3—BALANCE

Fatigue invites stress. It can be either physical or mental. Mental is the worst. But here we have a truly proven solution. It is simply to reorder your daily life into approximate thirds—one-third for productive work, one-third for rest, and one-third *to recreate your whole person*. The third one-third can take many forms, from contemplation or stargazing all the way to several hours of vigorous physical exercise (see APPROACH 8). It is your choice. Clearly exercise can bring about a very significant tranquilizing effect without the potential adverse side-effects of a prescription. Medical science has, of course, developed some ideal age norms concerning exercise duration, intensity, and target heartbeat rates—about which you should consult your physician.

APPROACH 4—SIMPLIFY

In answer to the nagging question, "Why is it that the busiest people get everything done, while the rest of us drown in half finished projects, despairing over all those things we meant to do but didn't?" Even *Parade Magazine* found the experts in agreement that:

- We fail to set priorities.
- We procrastinate.
- We bite off more than we can chew.
- We try to do everything perfectly.[6]

Various authors and time management experts have treated this subject in a wide variety of ways, but here are some fairly commonplace—yet invaluable—suggestions on which there appears to be general agreement:

- Establish priorities.
- Plan your time.
- Follow the plan.
- Do the most dreaded thing first.
- Reduce your possessions and trappings.
- Do not flit from unfinished task to unfinished task.
- Try to handle each item of paper only once.
- Make use of the knowledge of others.
- Delegate more.
- Start each day fresh—no animosities or grudges.
- Above all, learn to say no.

APPROACH 5—REALITY

Unrealistic expectations can only postpone or compound the ultimate trauma of a bad situation. Nearly everyone knows from experience that, to attract attention, it is hard to beat a big fat mistake. Reality says deal with it immediately.

[6] Lou Ann Walker, "How to Make Time Work for You," *Parade Magazine* (May 10, 1987), p. 4.

Expect frailty in others. Although we learned this in Chapter 4, nothing can be more disconcerting or stressful than for a heretofore trustworthy and dependable associate to fail to perform or fail to honor a previous commitment. Yet it happens with regularity and should not be viewed with surprise. In our nation's space program it is called "having a backup system," and we do have them even for the most sophisticated and reliable hardware. Why should it be any different for the most complex unit of all: the human being?

Stress is also produced in a CEO when he realizes that some under his command are unhappy. But the epitome of unreality is to suppose even for an instant that your job is to make everyone happy all the time. Relax! You cannot make even one individual happy all the time. Your own stress level will be lowered materially when you finally learn to strive for a more realistic morale "batting average" most of the time. It is the famous Menninger Clinic in Topeka, Kansas, that teaches executives—and especially parents—to be more "tolerant of ambiguity" and that "cognitive dissidence" (awareness of negative conditions) can be a powerful spur for maximum performance.

Moreover, it is most unrealistic to expect all organizational areas to be functioning effectively at all times. The executive who knows better has eliminated a common source of stress.

Finally, it is only realistic to expect the performance of a job to consume the exact length of time available. How often we find that otherwise competent people will procrastinate to the very end, when they know the deadline in advance. No need for stress. EXPECT IT!

APPROACH 6—RELEASE

One of the most valuable lessons the author has learned from experience came in the latter half of his 40 years in business, to wit: THE MERE PASSAGE OF 24 HOURS CAN THROW AN ENTIRELY NEW LIGHT ON A PROBLEM THAT CLAMORED FOR DECISION ONLY YESTERDAY.

Early in one's career the compulsion to act can be overwhelming. Yet efficient decision making can sometimes add to stress, when a more deliberate strategy would have reduced or perhaps even eliminated it altogether.

When there is little time left to deliberate and night falls, remember that the subconscious mind never gets tired or sleeps. Even when you are completely exhausted physically the *Daily Word* recommends "a proven and much advised treatment for stress-related" challenges. The method involves "talking" the body into relaxing by starting at the top of the head, as follows:

> I calm my mind and relax. I can feel a warm glow of relaxation flowing over me. It starts at the top of my head, moves over my shoulders and down my back to my legs and feet. My arms become relaxed and hang loose. My lungs breathe deep and even breaths. My heart beats in perfect rhythm. My digestive system is relaxed and quiet. Now, I am totally and completely relaxed.[7]

At this point, give it a try. Turn the stress-laden problem over to your tireless subconscious mind. Nothing to lose. You really might be surprised at what you will be able to write down about your problem the next morning.

Perhaps there is a way to demonstrate once and for all the incredible reach and practical value of *harnessing your subconscious mind power*. It's simple. It's quick. It may serve you well.

We all know the frustration of mislaying important papers, jewelry, notes, numbers, and so forth. When you have tried all else, *write down what you need to find*. Then, just before drifting off to sleep for the night, COMMAND YOUR SUBCONSCIOUS MIND TO HAVE THE ANSWER FOR YOU IN THE MORNING. You may be amazed at the results—and especially its increasing reliability.

According to a late 1987 issue of *Soundings,* the popular actress, entrepreneur, and author Arlene Dahl has contrived her own variation, a New Year's resolution technique. On every January 1, she writes down everything she would truly like to change in her life and seals it in an envelope, not to be opened until July 1. What a pleasant surprise at mid-year to her to find she can cross off quite a few of them that her subconscious mind has automatically worked

---

[7] *Daily Word,* (October 1987), p. 20. Used with permission of Unity School of Christianity, Publishers of DAILY WORD, Unity Village, Missouri, 64065.

on successfully in the meantime. As for the others, they just go back in the drawer for another six months.[8]

APPROACH 7—SELFLESSNESS

In those "new officer" meetings mentioned in Chapter 5, another key question I always used to ask—and I must admit it's a little tricky—was, *"What do you consider your job to be?"* Invariably for nearly 20 years each new officer would specify in detail his or her duties very clearly. But *only once* in that time did a new officer say, "And a big part of my job is to help others grow."

Fortunately it came in one of the early years, which enabled me to make the point solidly every year thereafter. Ultimately it gave birth to the word GROWTH-SHARING, now a true *way of life* for the entire institution. I commend growth-sharing to you, especially when you feel yourself stressed by your own circumstances. Learn first hand the inner reward of losing one's self in the process of enhancing the professional growth of another—a proven approach to stress reduction.

APPROACH 8—EXERCISE

When all else fails, stress relief is often obtainable almost immediately through exercise. The vigor and intensity, of course, should vary with the individual because an overdose will almost always be counterproductive and will only intensify anxiety during the necessary resting period.

One noted authority contends that proper exercise releases a "morphine-like" substance in the brain and throughout the nervous system after "prolonged exercise" of 40 or more minutes, the result of which is a sedative effort for several hours.[9] It also is a known fact that professional athletes have lower heart rates and blood pressure levels than stress-prone individuals.

But the most pronounced positive effect, in the author's experience, is the plain *sense of well-being* once the mind is totally

---

[8] Arlene Dahl, actress and author, *Soundings,* vol. 3 no. 2, (1987), p. 8.

[9] *Executive Health Report* XXIV, no. 4, P.O. Box 8880, Chapel Hill, N.C., 27515.

focused on the exercise itself, especially if a sport or skill is involved. Be aware, however, that exercise can actually become addictive. It should never be allowed to put job, family, or health in jeopardy.

LOSE A JOB—GAIN A CAREER

Of course, one of the most common sources of stress is the sudden loss of employment. Inasmuch as the average tenure of a chief executive has been estimated to be less than five years (depending on the industry), this chapter would be glaringly incomplete without a word on this dreaded subject.

But it need not be dreaded.

Think of the people you know who would be better off physically, mentally, emotionally, and perhaps even financially if engaged in a different job or profession.

Is your own name on the list? Think about it. Is it the change or merely the *adjustment period* that disturbs you? A recent issue of the *American Banker* contained this testimonial of Merri Rosenberg:

> The experience of losing a job affects people differently—and their response to the pursuit of a new position differs accordingly. Following are the experiences of two individuals, neither of whom started out as bankers, who landed on their feet in a bank after losing a job in another industry.
>
> For a former advertising executive, losing her job "was an opportunity to reassess" what she had been doing and reevaluate where she intended to take her career. Her advice:
> - Remain positive. It's not always horrible to lose your job.
> - Do all the things they tell you to do in outplacement, but pick and choose what seems most beneficial.
> - Like anything else you do, listen to what seems helpful.
> - Network a lot. I did it myself, and it paid off.
>
> The other individual, a 20-year veteran of a manufacturing concern who lost his job when the conglomerate decided to spinoff his division, acknowledges that being fired was "very stressful. I had my income and family to worry about." As he puts it, "I had worked for more than 21 years at a company, and felt like a failure that it

didn't work out in the end. The good thing about going through outplacement was it helped me get my feelings off my chest."

Outplacement helped him realize that losing his job was not entirely his fault and that political problems within the company, as well as external economic pressure, had put him in that situation.

Outplacement counseling ultimately helped him choose between two job offers, as well as determine his long-term career path.[10]

Who knows. The loss of a job—however stressful it may be—could turn out to be the key to your ultimate career. Besides, you now have something in common with Lee Iacocca!

THE MOOD METER

Nearly 30 years ago I stumbled onto Dr. Hornell Hart's fascinating book, *Autoconditioning: the New Way to a Successful Life*.[11] Although it was not at all intended as a self-help substitute for one's religious commitment, I am thoroughly convinced that this little book can lift the spiritual quality of almost anyone's life—not to mention the economic quality. We shall reproduce only the MOOD METER here (figure 8), together with its "instructions for use in eight steps" (figure 9). The use of such a scorecard for reducing stress—or, indeed, living on the plus side of the MOOD METER—would seem to make a lot of good sense.

ARE GURUS NOW OUT?

We close this chapter tongue-in-cheek, but who knows where the idea of having a brain tune-up may be headed (no pun).

According to the *Wall Street Journal*, "high strung people" are now on the threshold of being able to buy "inner peace for a

---

[10] Merri Rosenberg, "Easing the Blow to Fired Workers," *American Banker*, (March 19, 1987), p. 4.

[11] Hornell Hart, Ph.D., *AUTOCONDITIONING: The New Way to a Successful Life* (Reprinted by permission of the publisher, Prentice Hall, Inc., Englewood Cliffs, N.J., 1956), pp. 5–7.

	Hour													
MOOD-METER / Day														
15 Ecstatic														
14 Triumphant														
13 Jubilant														
12 Elated														
11 Delighted														
10 Joyful														
9 Gay														
8 Lighthearted														
7 Happy														
6 Pleased														
5 Satisfied														
4 Encouraged														
3 Cheerful														
2 Purposeful														
1 Determined														
0														
-1 Anxious														
-2 Worried														
-3 Lonely														
-4 Frustrated														
-5 Upset														
-6 Disillusioned														
-7 Downcast														
-8 Gloomy														
-9 Downhearted														
-10 Discouraged														
-11 Disgusted														
-12 Depressed														
-13 Desperate														
-14 Despairing														
-15 Miserable														
Top plus number Lowest minus no.														
Sum = score														

Figure 8

INSTRUCTIONS FOR USE OF MOOD-METER

1. Enter at the top of the first column the day and the hour at which you are taking the test.
2. Put a check mark opposite each word that you feel fairly sure describes the way you feel at the time. Check all the happy words and all the unhappy ones that really are correct for your present mood. Always be sincere when you check the list; otherwise you will destroy the value of this instrument for you.
3. Note the number at the left of the highest word above 0 that you have checked on the list. Enter that number in the space opposite the words, "Top plus number" at the bottom of the Mood-Meter. If the top word that you checked has a minus number, enter 0 here.
4. Do the same for the number of the lowest word that you have checked below 0 on the list, entering this with a minus sign opposite the words, "Lowest minus number." If you checked no word below 0, enter 0 here.
5. Now find the sum of these two numbers. If one number is positive and the other negative, the smaller number must be subtracted from the larger one; and the difference must take the sign of the larger number. The answer is your mood-score. Put a circle (0) at the level of that score.
6. Put the Mood-Meter aside. Then, a few hours or maybe a day later, when your mood has changed, take the test again.
7. When you have entered the circle to represent your new score, connect that by a straight line to your old circle in order to show your trend.
8. Especially when you feel "up" or "down" in your mood, take the test again.

Figure 9

mere $10" per visit.[12] Patrons of Transcendental Meditation—because it "takes too long"—are now opting for "hooking themselves up to a device called a *Synchro-Energizer,* which is supposed to "tune up" the wavelengths of the brain. The machine costs about $50,000 and can accommodate up to 32 "serenity seekers" at a time. A "piece of nirvana" is yours in no more than 45 minutes. The Synchro-Energizer is the brainchild (no pun) of Denis Gorges, a Cleveland psychiatrist. He says he spent about 30 years developing it, and he is clearly elated with the volunteered testimonials it has generated (no pun, really). Satisfied users espouse a "tremendous desire for self-improvement."

Stick around, friends, for more stimulating (pun intended) news on this—shall we say—"short circuit" to a stress-free world!

REMEMBER YOUR ROOTS

Another occupational snare of the successful executive is the *grandeur* that almost inevitably comes with reaching the top. Few escape its magnetic allure, and, ironically, those with the most modest beginnings are usually the ones who most easily succumb to a not-so-shy lifestyle. A good form of therapy is *going home again*—I mean all the way back to one's *roots*. In fact, the sense of calm and the warm glow of achievement it produces are strong nourishment for the psyche—whether you happen to be a proud CEO or not.

My niece, Barbara McLean, a successful travel agent on the West Coast, made her pilgrimage last summer back to Storm Lake, Iowa. No family is left there and only one or two acquaintances. But Barbara was determined to have one more look at the family's old homestead. She had made connecting flights to Sioux City and had rented a car there. It was not easy nor was it anything like the way she usually spent her vacations. But the glow on her face, as she told me about it later, was several shades brighter than when she had described her various cruises and trips abroad. In her case, no grandeur remedies were needed. But as I thought about it later, what a great way to keep things in clear perspective—and who among us cannot use an extra measure of that now and then?

---

[12] Carrie Dolan, "Try a Brain Tuneup," *Wall Street Journal,* (October 21, 1987), p. 6.

STRESS: NOT YET AN "ENDANGERED SPECIES"

Because stress is likely to remain with us for a very long time, no one should expect to escape it altogether. It is far better to confront it headlong with the realization that we don't get ulcers from what we eat, but rather from what's "eating us."

A bonus chapter and Epilogue follow. The latter is written essentially for the purpose of presenting some of the clear and costly *trade-offs*—whether stressful or not—involved in serving as a chief executive, in return for its *unique rewards*.

Chapter 11

BONUS CHAPTER: UNDERSTANDING WHY BOSSES FAIL

You never know what you can do until you try to undo what you did.
—Anonymous

A QUICK DISCLAIMER

Any relationship between this bonus chapter—11—and the "Chapter 11" remedy in bankruptcy is unintended and completely coincidental. Suffice it to say that whether a chief executive ever experiences a near brush with financial failure or not, his or her basic understanding of the snares and pitfalls that have claimed others will be invaluable.

WHY CHAPTER 11?

As indicated in the preface, this book's first ten chapters and its epilogue are about CEO preparation and competence, essentially for the benefit of those aspiring to become chief executives; hence its title: *So You Want to Be the Boss?*

But effective performance in the top job—once in office—is every bit as challenging, if not even more illusive. Indeed, no treatise on "becoming the boss" would do genuine justice to the subject without a realistic assessment of some of the more common *causes of failure* and oft repeated *mistakes to be avoided,* especially those that have cost incumbents their jobs. *Fifteen basic managerial mistakes* are presented here, together with the author's comments concerning real life examples of each.

ON BEING A SECURE WINNER

Some would say that studying the misdeeds that contributed to the failure of others is a debilitating exercise and even risks—subconsciously at least—the adoption of the dreaded *loser's mentality.* A bevy of management consultants, whose primary mission is to counsel executives to "tune out fears of failure, are readily available for hire."[1]

For almost all of my 40 years in management, the indelible *positive thinking* thesis of Norman Vincent Peale[2] and the popular ballad of a generation ago, "*Accentuate the Positive,*" left little room for studying failure. I remember, too, a profound line from a *hot book* in the mid-fifties by Walter Germain: "*the positive must dominate, the negative must be quelled.*"[3]

More recently, however, from the relaxed clarity of retirement, I am now persuaded—unalterably, in fact—that one of the most positive steps one can take is to have sufficient *inner security* to learn from the mistakes of others and to apply what is learned. Instinctively, I used to think that it was *treacherous to focus on how others stumbled,* feeling—unlike the flighty moth—that if I didn't get *near the flame, I wouldn't get burned.*

These are only clichés to me now. Why else would great golfers spend hours on trouble shots—and they all do. They do it because they have found that proficiency in a bunker with the sand wedge is the very antidote for the poisonous fear of hitting the ball

---

[1] Denis E. Waitley, Ph.D., *Psychology of Winning* (Chicago: Nightengale-Conant Corporation, 1988), Tape No. 2.

[2] Norman Vincent Peale, *The Power of Positive Thinking* (Englewood Cliffs, N.J.: Prentice-Hall, Inc., 1952).

[3] Walter M. Germain, *The Magic Power of Your Mind* (New York: Hawthorn Books Inc., 1956), p. 156.

there in the first place. Does a sailing instructor teach only on calm waters? Does anyone even learn to drive a car safely without knowing what to do in an emergency?

In short, it is now my clear conviction that it is not at all a too negative approach to investigate reasons *why bosses fail*. There will be plenty of time to "tune them out" later.

THE DON'TS REVISITED

Back in Chapter 2,[4] each of the forty DON'TS was derived from real life mistakes that I either made myself or witnessed; but, as I recall, not one of them by itself left the offender unemployed.

Since composing the first draft of *So You Want to Be the Boss?*, the DON'TS have been "classroom tested." The author has, in fact, *survived* three semesters as an ad hoc professor for Managerial Leadership 4710–002,[5] using the book as its text. In discussing the DON'TS with students, the inevitable question was: "What happens when CEOs violate one of them?" Then, as the *war stories* followed, it became clear to me (as never before) that among some of the casualty cases I had known it had taken only two or three DON'TS in habitual combination to cost the transgressor his job. Such is the peril of being the boss. But there must be a better way to organize and understand *why bosses fail*.

THE MPM REVISITED

There *is* a better way and it, too, is reminiscent of Chapter 2. As the reader may recall, the first column of the MASTER PLANNING MODEL (MPM), RESEARCH, had four subheadings—*economic, market, organizational,* and *other*—with all GOAL SETTING based upon fact finding in these four areas. Amazingly, as I began to organize the *fifteen basic managerial mistakes* that follow, it struck me that they too can appropriately be classified by the same four headings.

---

[4] See page 21.
[5] College of Business Administration, University of Oklahoma.

For example, the first three of our faulty fifteen are *economic* in nature (basic economic blunders that, in effect, amounted to failure on the part of the chief executive); 4 through 6 are *market* related (examples of how costly it can be when the boss ignores marketing fundamentals); numbers 7 through 10 involve *organizational* considerations (the importance of relating corporate strategies to strengths and weaknesses—financial and otherwise—of the organizational structure); and, finally the remaining five are associated with a variety of *other* factors (each with its own separate identity such as *faulty vision, questionable ethics, misdirected goals*). Undoubtedly, these examples will call to the reader's mind a myriad of similar examples of others who stumbled in almost exactly the same manner.

FIFTEEN FATAL FAILURES

1. **Failure to perceive the secular trend:** XYZ Home Ice Service[6] was a regional leader years ago in basic *residential refrigeration*. Its market share was dominant in six or seven nearby communities for the manufacture and delivery of ice (and iceboxes).
   Fatal flaw? Its primary service and product lines—while "cash cows" for years—were to have little following later, as more sophisticated electrical refrigeration emerged.
   Commentary: Unlike dozens of entrepreneurs in the "ice/icebox" business who became early and very successful electrical appliance dealers, the head of XYZ, one of the community's strongest leaders, never saw the economic inevitability of the *long-term trend* in the business that he had founded and he failed to modify the mix of its product line or service. I watched it sadly decline, slowly at first during the mid-1930s but, by about 1940, the business had literally melted away. XYZ might well have survived by considering itself in the *refrigeration* business rather than the *ice* business. Other such casualties familiar to all include (of course) the *buggy whip*, the *typewriter*, and *passenger railroads*, each a victim of failing to

---

[6] For obvious reasons, the names of the businesses involved will remain anonymous, hence the XYZ pseudonyms.

perceive their own *secular trends* or to realize what business they were really in.

2. **Failure to recognize the cyclical trend:** XYZ Fashions of Dallas had developed a statewide following as a leader in *ladies high fashion apparel*. It had even been mentioned by one national publication as a contender for regional style-setting honors.

   Fatal flaw? Its expensive popular product lines were vastly overstocked and inventories were bulging well beyond the capacity of a flat to downward market to absorb, just when the economic *business cycle* of the region turned negative.

   Commentary: A vain and overconfident management, blinded by its trendy publicity, narrowly escaped closing its doors when it failed to heed a well-publicized correction cycle in oil and gas prices. How quickly such *cyclical trends* can erode sales volume of luxury items especially in a single-industry–based economy, no matter how successful the establishment has been in headier days.

3. **Failure to respect the seasonal trend:** XYZ Foods was a borrowing customer of our bank during its formative years. The superior reputation for *premium meats* that it earned over the years had been good for its widening profit margin.

   Fatal flaw? Because of its dominant market share, management was unconcerned with the subtle effect of the *seasonality* of a growing proportion of the company's product line.

   Commentary: While a more sophisticated and discriminating public was learning about *specialty foods* for warmer weather, with little aversion to their higher price tags, a preoccupied and complacent management failed to adjust its product line accordingly. Three years of *seasonality* cut annual revenues nearly in half, requiring an unwanted consolidation in order to bail out pressing financial difficulties.

4. **Failure to remain abreast of technology and its dynamic effect upon competitive product design:** XYZ Telecommunications was led during the 1960s by a tough-minded accountant who delivered 58 straight quarters of earnings growth.

   Fatal flaw? Almost oblivious to *chip* technology that would spell the demise of the older *analog* system, management elected to forego the expense of *market research* in favor of a rash of worldwide acquisitions.

Commentary: Trained observers now say that attempts to improvise and compensate for the basic error of ignoring *technological changes* in the company's marketplace have permanently cost this giant a chance for real leadership in telecommunications. While I only witnessed this one from a disinterested vantage point, it really stressed the indispensability of *market research,* even for the giants, especially those whose fortunes are inextricably tied to technological advancement.

5. **Failure to monitor competition:** XYZ Motors, always concerned with its so-called market penetration, was an industry leader in offering options to a fickle public, so much so that no competitor in the early 1950s could begin to match XYZ's more than 900 combinations of alternate specifications in its mid-range priced automobile. Our bank and the automobile industry were only a fountain pen apart. Such was our interest in quality installment loans.

    Fatal flaw? XYZ and other giants of the industry, apparently so impressed with their attempts to saturate the market with "customer choices," failed to focus on the lowest end of their product mix. The Italian Fiat, the German Volkswagen, and later the Japanese Toyota and Datsun were to gain entry and—*without offering any options at all*—began grinding out a single product and made it better and cheaper each thousand units.

    Commentary: How wrong it was for the big car makers to refuse to recognize the size and need of the low end of the market, the alternative to the used car. For it was here in the late 1950s and 1960s that single-minded foreign manufacturers were able to establish themselves as both *cheaper* and *better* builders of transportation, a perception that serves them well today at all price levels. I learned, as I saw it all take place, that even the most successful can ill afford to ignore competition at whatever level it occurs.

6. **Failure to make a distinction between tangible products and intangible services:** XYZ Stores was one of the first to launch in-store financial centers in 1982. The idea was to sell its "one-stop customers" such things as homes, securities, mortgages,

The MPM Revisited

CDs, personal loans, and credit cards with checking privileges.

Fatal flaw? Selling stocks next to socks just didn't make it. Similarly, financial service sales simply failed to follow walking traffic density patterns. People just didn't treat their individual banking needs with the same degree of casualness as getting something for the kitchen.

Commentary: Attempting to deliver financial services through nontraditional channels fails to delineate between *tangible products* and *intangible services*. For example, XYZ learned the hard way that 80 percent to 90 percent of business with a securities broker is conducted by telephone. What is still unresolved, however, is whether or not a *free-standing financial service shopping center* would be a more effective delivery system than the general retailing-financial service combination. This way, people seeking financial services would not need to battle crowds usually associated with retail stores. "Free-standing financial service shopping center"—what a mouthful. My own view is that the single word "bank" would do very nicely, if only Congress would finally *level the regulatory playing field for banks and non-banks*.

7. **Failure to maintain a strong organizational structure:** The XYZ Tool & Dye Company was well entrenched in its industry with a relatively stable product/service mix presented to the trade in eight cities between Houston and Denver. It had enjoyed a respectable, albeit flat, earning power for nearly ten years. In mid-year 1960, an exclusive new product line virtually took off in sales and an immediate and growing backlog of orders resulted from its almost overwhelming customer acceptance.

Fatal flaw? XYZ's *table of organization* had never been complete and the sudden windfall of new business quickly made it necessary for quite a number of the veteran employees to take on extra duties. As XYZ's loan officer for our bank, I watched management let this crisis condition—though highly profitable—go on much too long and ultimately lead to a complete turnover of the management team.

Commentary: The absence of a carefully constructed organization chart with a mechanism for its periodic improvement is a serious management omission. Pressing busy personnel into functions for which they are untrained is rarely satisfactory for long and often can be counterproductive in terms of staff *overload,* unwanted *attrition* and, more seriously, *inept performance.*

8. **Failure to substitute participative management (PM) for the top-down decision-making style of yesteryear:** XYZ Building Supply Stores was a genuine Horatio Alger success story. It was begun more than 40 years ago by its founder—and only chief executive. He was what some called a "benevolent despot"—shrewd and calculating in making the right business decisions for the stores, handling almost every management detail personally. He was completely condescending, in a lovable sort of way, to everyone around him. But, since everyone knew and accepted J.P.'s unique style for what it was, XYZ Stores flourished and had expanded into five states before he died at 83.

    Fatal flaw? Upon the death of the founder and the selection of a third-generation family successor who quickly tried to emulate his style—why not? everyone was accustomed to it—there was a downward spiral in morale that nearly killed the company. Only an unwanted takeover 18 months later stemmed the hemorrhage of resignations by key old-timers, who simply weren't up for more of the same *autocratic* treatment they had somehow stomached from the founder, but were unwilling to endure from his grandson.

    Commentary: An interesting and quite predictable study in human nature. The founder's management style was clearly *obsolete* (see Chapter 2, *The Obsolete Manager*), but he succeeded in spite of it. Regrettably, however, he also excelled in welling up an enormous wall of pent-up frustration ready to burst when, even at his death, there was still no opportunity to *participate in the decision-making process.* Too bad the young legacy successor was insufficiently enlightened to know how much more effectively he could have taken charge, with a carefully orchestrated format of *participative goal setting—*both *organizational* and *personal* (see Chapter 4, Inward Marketing).

9. **Failure to reject greed:** XYZ Drilling Company, although only marginally capitalized, managed to sustain stable and attrac-

The MPM Revisited

tive earnings during the early 1950s through large short-term borrowings from our bank, secured by major oil company accounts receivable. Its four oil and gas drilling rigs were fully financed by a leading supply company, with a resulting long-term "debt to worth ratio" of about 10 to 1—lots of leverage for a small drilling company, wholly owned by its founder.

Fatal flaw? It took only a cool breeze in the energy economy to drop XYZ's net revenues below the level needed to service its mountain of debt. The bank was out in about a hundred days as the receivables liquidated, but the supply company was stuck with the rigs for over a year and our sole owner lost his entire equity investment.

Commentary: The dangers of the heavy leveraging of debt when a downturn comes are well documented in all fields. The shortsightedness—indeed, the greed—of ambitious owners, who are reluctant to give up ownership in exchange for a more stable capital base (see Chapter 6, Ownership Myopia), can so easily result in their entire invested capital being wiped out. If only they could settle for a lesser ownership in the beginning by financing the business with *invested dollars* from partners, rather than the *borrowed dollars* of creditors, which can only be repaid from prolonged periods of uninterrupted profits.

10. **Failure to respect debt:** One of my neighbors, back in Houston days, was the successful founder and sole owner of XYZ Scope, Inc. Its patented process had earned a virtually exclusive niche in the oil patch and—conservatively—Dave's net worth had grown to more than $12 million in about ten years.

Fatal flaw? Around five o'clock one warm Saturday afternoon, I was down at the pool alone when Dave arrived (not his real name) with not one but two double scotch and sodas. As he handed one to me, he said, "I've just got to talk about it! . . . I know you're going to share my excitement!" With that, he proceeded to tell me that he wanted to pledge up to half his XYZ stock for a $4½ million dollar loan from our bank to buy the old World War II Liaison Aircraft Company (not the real name) and that it would be easy enough to augment the $30,000 plane's radio and navigation equipment for less than $50,000 each and preempt the business executive market with a private four-passenger carrier priced under $100,000, capable of six hours aloft and a cruising speed of 180 knots. "Besides," he added with great fervor, "I just *love* this airplane!"

Commentary: At about this point—realizing that XYZ paid no dividends and that such a loan could be paid only by the sale of assets, or an immediately successful venture into a highly speculative new field, all financed by otherwise unmanageable heavy indebtedness—I decided to pour my scotch and soda into the pool.

The smile on Dave's face gradually began to fade as I said with as much empathy as I could, "Dave, because we're both good neighbors and good friends, I'm going to level with you. If instead of saying you '*loved it*,' you had said you 'almost *hated* this aircraft, but here's why it can't miss,' I might have listened more closely, but this loan has no primary source of repayment (much less secondary), except through distressed sale of stock of one or both of the companies. In short, Dave, to finance your excitement for this plane, yet to be modified, *all on borrowed money* with no certain plan of repayment simply does not meet our bank's basic lending policy requirements, and it would not be a true act of friendship on my part to go along with this deal."

After more conversation, he said he understood, but I was skeptical.

Although Dave and I remained friends, a competitor bank soon made the loan and captured both the XYZ and Liaison Aircraft banking relationships—not a very happy outcome of our neighborly visit at the pool. But, in just 14 months, Liaison was struggling and deeply in the red; Dave had suffered a massive heart attack and lost controlling ownership of both companies. Of course, his health might have failed whether he "loved the Liaison Aircraft" and borrowed all that money or not. But I will probably always feel that a healthier *respect for debt*—and what constitutes manageable debt—might have prolonged my neighbor's business success and his health as well.

11. **Failure to develop a balanced vision for the business:** The XYZ Bank & Trust Company was a stodgy, but highly respected, third-generation bank in a prosperous county seat town in east

Texas. Because it made few loans, a disproportionate share of its resources were invested in long-term government securities. Accordingly, the father and son management team devoted at least half their office hours to discussing and/or trading government bonds for the bank's account.

Fatal flaw? Both finally succumbed to the same compulsive trading allure that has taken its toll so savagely in the commodity markets. Part of the seduction, of course, was the heady feeling of controlling and moving around all those millions, even though most of them belonged to the depositors. The part that belonged to them, as shareholders, was ultimately wiped out when long-term bond rates peaked at nearly 16% in the fall of 1981. With each new high in rates, bond values of course declined and the bank's precious liquidity was further eroded in favor of purchasing a still longer maturity at a new high yield. When the aggregate cost of the portfolio exceeded its market value by more than the bank's capital funds, regulators had no choice but to close the bank—effectively wiping out the owners—and find a nearby successor bank to salvage the remains of what had once been a landmark institution.

Commentary: The prudent policy of guarding the quality of its loans by simply saying "No" in slow business periods had served the owners well, indeed, better than the community. But to go to the other extreme by making massive long-term commitments in bonds whose value tumbled when rates of interest made their historic climb was a fatal blunder. A more *balanced vision* of the bank's role as both a constructive *lender* (protector of *liquidity*) and controlled bond *investor* would almost certainly have saved the day.

12. **Failure to harness vision:** XYZ-TECH, Inc. was still in its infancy, only 18 months in business. It was reasonably well financed by high-risk venture capitalists and its pending patents promised large new money management benefits to the consumer. The chief executive, a truly inventive entrepreneur, envisioned an outright sale of the company to one of three nationwide financial service giants. His vision was closed to any other course of action.

    Fatal flaw? In another time, perhaps no flaw at all. That's right, this single-minded maverick might well have made it big in one giant step. Large achievements begin with large dreams. But if I could coin a new word that best fits this case, it would be *"hypervisionary"* (not to be found in your dictionary). My definition would be: *"an excessively unrealistic image of future prospects."* And so it was with XYZ-TECH. The leader's determination to make the *big hit* brought the company to its knees financially.

Commentary: As this is written, however, all is not lost for XYZ-TECH. The chief executive has finally *harnessed his vision;* the *giant sale* is on hold; and a *pilot test* of one of the company's major products is being negotiated with a progressive local bank—all just in time, hopefully, to launch a successful shareholder assessment for necessary capital funds. It has been said that: *"Sometimes, worse than being wrong is being right too soon."*[7] Indeed, it's hard enough to be *right* at all, but it's all the more crucial to possess a good *sense of timing* for necessary preliminary steps. Let's call it *harnessing one's vision*—no matter how worthy or ambitious it may have been—in favor of more practical and realistic approaches.

13. **Failure to observe the ethical dimension:** XYZ Motors had outgrown every other automobile dealer in the state and now—in its 25th year—was recognized as both the volume and service leader in the region for its well-established brands. Second-generation management was experienced and competent, with a good record of earnings and was a large user of our bank's floor plan line of credit.

Fatal flaw? A thoughtless *short cut* led to a buildup in exposed borrowings (that is, unsecured by a properly margined vehicle inventory), and, eventually, the line of credit was—as the bank examiners would say—"out of trust." This means: *too much owing on too few cars.* The *short cut* was simply not to worry about paying down the floor plan line of credit as cars were sold.

Commentary: This of course created both an *overextended* debt position and a *false sense of liquidity* in the cash account, which was unfortunately used for extravagant purposes. One

---

[7] William Taylor, Federal Reserve System, *ABA Banking Journal* (1988), p. 3.

of those purposes was a headstrong investment in real estate which, in turn, led to a strained financial condition that finally resulted in cancellation of the bank's line of credit and involuntary liquidation of the business. What a different scenario it might have been if, instead of the early *short cut,* XYZ Motors management had been more attentive to the *ethical dimension* of its business. However prevalent the "out of trust" problem is among dealers, no amount of finger pointing at others who operate unethically can excuse even a single departure from scrupulous honesty in all business dealings. Indeed, Mark Twain was so wrong when he mused, "virtue has never been as respectable as money."[8]

14. **Failure to make the management/leadership distinction:** XYZ National Bank and ABC National Bank were heated rivals in a distant city. The gap between them in total resources had narrowed considerably by 1976, two years after the death of XYZ's dynamic leader and founder. The directors of XYZ—much the larger in 1974—had moved quickly to fill the vacancy by elevating the *trusted* and *ultraconservative* executive vice-president and controller. "He sure won't get us into trouble," was the rationale.

Fatal flaw? This well-meaning former middle manager was not just ultraconservative; he was also the *consumate pessimist.* I once heard him complain, "Why is it, as soon as you find the key to success—they change the locks?" His fellow officers knew him as "old hard-luck-Charlie." While Charlie was *managing* instead of *leading* (see Chapter 3, for *the difference*), ABC had caught XYZ from behind and, on a couple of "call dates," was in fact larger in both total resources and earnings.

Commentary: ABC National Bank's CEO was an acknowledged *leader* who had learned early on that the most effective way to advance his own career was to take the time to reach down and help others achieve their own brand of success. Five years earlier, he had installed both group and personal *goal-setting systems,* all geared to *incentive compensation,* for key executives. His participative style had worked well and the bank's effective team of executives grew larger each year, as

---

[8] Mark Twain, "Thoughts on the Business Life," *Forbes,* (January 23, 1989), p. 128.

ABC directors authorized expanding the system to include more and more participants. In reflecting upon the contrast of the two bank's working cultures, the value of making the *management/leadership distinction* certainly can be crucial in terms of an organization's competitive performance.

15. **Failure to understand the true definition of success:** The Chairman and CEO of XYZ Corp., a personal friend of mine since the late 1950s, had seemingly done nearly everything just right in the building of a then leading specialty foods conglomerate. The year was 1978. It had all been the result of his broad and incisive *vision* of both the industry and XYZ's particular *niche,* which he and his effective team of executives were able to fulfill with steadily growing profitability.

Fatal flaw? Upon reflection, my wealthy old friend—a recognized "captain of industry" about to break into the *Fortune Five Hundred*—was miserable! It was as though the previous two decades had been wasted in a *misdirected zeal* to achieve conventional material gain at the expense of all else. As a matter of fact, he had started out years before from one of the lowest rungs on the economic ladder—he had always been driven to amass as much wealth as he possibly could.

Commentary: The author knows of no survey yet contrived for identifying bosses whose eyes are "on the wrong ball" for achieving long-term success. If one is ever concocted, I'm sure its reliability will depend upon the extent to which the respondent is made to distinguish between *success* and *happiness.*

Columnist Berry Gordy, writing in *The New York Times* of January 14, 1979[9] summed it up quite well I think:

One of the most important problems in being an entrepreneur is the problem of happiness after success. Many people might say, "Hey Baby, give me the success, and I'll worry about the happiness afterwards." Unfortunately, it doesn't happen that way. Unless you consider happiness before you consider success, then the manner in which you achieve your success, will be something that will destroy you at some later date. Many people, in their rise to success, are so busy running to the top, stepping on their competitors, stepping on

---

[9] Used with permission of David Campbell, *If I'm In Charge Here, Why Is Everybody Laughing?* (Greensboro, N.C.: Center for Creative Leadership, 1984), p. 164.

their enemies and, saddest of all, stepping on their friends and loved ones that, when they get to the top, they look around and discover that they are extremely lonely and unhappy. They'll ask me, "Where did I go wrong?" My answer has always been: "Probably at the beginning."

What a pity the CEO of XYZ Corp., at his lowest rung on the ladder, never read Berry Gordy.

POOR PERSONNEL SELECTION: A ROOT CAUSE

Who is to say how many of the *fatal flaws*, at the root of these fifteen cases of failure by the boss, might have been avoided—or at least ameliorated—by early and better recruiting of more perceptive and more competent personnel. It has been my observation that some bosses not only don't *recruit* their top staff people very carefully, but neither do they *listen* to them when the "chips are down." One of the most capable executives I have known freely admits, "The problem of personnel selection is easily the most difficult problem, including financial problems, that I have ever had in running a business."[10]

PROCRASTINATION: A STILL DEADLY SIN

As if these *common failings* 1 through 15 were not enough to worry about in your climb to become *the boss*, the *deadly sin of procrastination*—thousands of years old—is just as treacherous as ever and can effectively kill your career before you ever get a chance to commit one of my *15 fatal failures*. Yet, at one time or another, the addiction of just plain *putting things off* touches nearly everyone.

From a recent survey, we have this finding:

Procrastination is one of the main factors that keeps an executive from moving up the corporate ladder. It's important that people handle tasks as they are dumped into their laps, instead of piling up more and more unfinished projects. We can avoid this rut by simply listing our priorities each day alphabetically; even with a list down to

[10] Jack H. Abernathy, former drilling contractor and utility executive.

"X," if we can only accomplish "A," "B" and "C" each day, most of us would lead incredibly happy lives."[11]

organize, Organize, ORGANIZE

Whether you use the ABC method, something from Sanskrit, or something from any other alphabet; the one sure remedy for procrastination is *organization*.

The criterion you choose by which to establish a priority for responding to heavy demands is secondary. You might decide to put *like problems* together . . . to group them according to the *estimated time* to be required . . . to organize for maximum *productivity* . . . or, as advocated in Chapter 2, to "do the *toughest thing* first." One final admonition: just be sure they're *your* "*things*" to do. Author Don Wright warns that the executive who is bogged down making decisions that subordinates should make is doomed to the fate of "a fireman rushing around from blaze to blaze."[12]

Of course at some point, you may become so organized that you will need to make a list of your lists, but at least when you get there—and all else has failed—you can always become an author!

THE DREADED RISK OF FAILURE KILLS TIME

Of course, one excuse for *procrastination* is the *risk of failure*—so we *coast* along in limbo much of the time. Yet, it's been the author's observation that the only way to *coast* is to go down hill. And the worst thing about that is the *waste of time*, while our *age* meters keep on ticking.

Frank Sinatra says, "Age improves wine, compound interest and nothing else I can think of . . . the one thing wrong with the younger generation is that a lot of us don't belong to it anymore."[13]

---

[11] Used with permission of Mrs. Mary Lou Lamphear, BSN, Paoli Hospital, Paoli, Pennsylvania. News Briefs, KTVY Channel 4, Oklahoma City, Oklahoma.

[12] Don Wright, *Moving Up from Indian to Chief* (Washington, D.C.: American Bankers Association, 1989) preliminary draft, chap. 2.

[13] Frank Sinatra, *Joey Adams Party Book* (West Palm Beach, Fla.: Globe Communications Corp., 1983), p. 64.

FAILING REALLY ISN'T ALL BAD

If the reader will reflect for a moment upon his or her own life long *triumphs* and *failures,* can't we agree that—as discouraging as they were—we almost always *learned more* from the *failures?* Indeed, when one learns from *failure,* the word *failure* itself literally disappears like magic, but it's not magic at all. *You see leaders don't do magic. Instead, they merely understand certain proven leadership principles, and they use certain basic leadership skills—and one such skill is to learn from failure.*

- Baseball legend, Babe Ruth, *struck out 1,330 times,* but he hit a record 714 home runs.
- Thomas A. Edison freely spoke of his more than *3,000 laboratory experiments that failed* before he finally invented the incandescent lamp.[14]
- John Kreese, prolific author of more than 500 novels, tells his friends that his works never would have come off the press without the nearly *700 rejection slips* from which he learned so much.
- Tennessee Williams[15] has said that without having suffered a *huge failure on his first play,* he would never have written *Glass Menagerie.*[16]
- Mr. A. Lincoln was *defeated eleven times* for public office.

So go ahead—before *aging* becomes your own form of failure—and take some (I believe the term is) *calculated risks.* After all, where is the *victory,* when there's *no risk of failure?* And when you risk and lose—everyone does, you know—remember that only

---

[14] Thomas Alva Edison, *Encyclopedia Britannica* (Chicago: William Benton, 1962), Volume 7, p. 962.

[15] Hyatt & Gottlieb, *When Smart People Fail* (New York: Penguin Books, 1988), p. 234.

[16] More about *leadership principles* and *leadership skills* will be contained in my next book, *Leaders Don't Do Magic,* which is already in outline form and will be co-authored by William F. Weitzel, Ph.D., Professor of Management, University of Oklahoma.

the most *vain* among us refuse to *admit* failure and only the most *insecure* among us refuse to forgive themselves for it, while only those who have learned the value of *instant admission* and *renewed self-acceptance* can experience that powerful surge of calm *confidence* and steady *determination* so necessary to risk again—and, this time, TO WIN.

EPILOGUE

Maybe—for you—it's just not worth it.
—Anonymous

After 11 consecutive chapters—each laden with its own ominous checklists of imperatives—the reader by now must be succumbing to second thoughts about reaching for the CEO ring.

But wait.

Being a chief executive does have its *compensations,* and that's precisely the word for it.

The prominent executive-recruiting firm, Heidrick & Struggles, Inc., recently reported a revealing "new study" of 897 leading corporate CEOs (approximately 25 percent responding).

Findings include a typical profile:

- A 58-year-old male who has been with his company 24 years; he is still married to his first spouse, but has not stayed with his first job.
- He makes big money; average cash compensation comes to $590,000, up 25 percent from 1984; some 9 percent earn more than $1 million annually versus only 3 percent three years ago.

- Forty-four percent have management contracts, and two-thirds of those have so-called "golden parachutes" (lucrative severance clauses) in the event of a merger.[1]

Admittedly, "lots of meeting time is involved"—an average of 17.3 hours a week with 6.3 hours of preparation time, and the normal work week averages a heavy 61.1 hours with only two to three weeks of vacation annually. These massive commitments of time and energy by these leading CEOs serve to introduce our final area of inquiry. Let's call it *the costly trade-offs involved in serving as a chief executive in return for the unique rewards*.

Considerable time and thought were devoted by the author to the order of presentation (according to the relative "downside pull") of each item "traded off." While few remained in the original sequence on subsequent runs, there was one that consistently led them all. We open with it.

TRADE-OFF NUMBER ONE—FAMILY

The high price paid in terms of time lost with spouse and family is uniformly acknowledged. Some say it is virtually impossible to achieve an acceptable balance. One prominent young CEO recently said publicly, "After a business trip of two weeks or so, it takes me about four days to reestablish myself with my four-year-old, and that hurts."

He was right. The benefits of a *strong family life* must be earned. But the task is not hopeless. Some of the busiest executives I have known also have had strong family orientations. Guarding the weekends and avoiding night work rank high among their prerequisites for avoiding Trade-off Number One.

TRADE-OFF NUMBER TWO—STUDY

Contrary to popular belief, the effective CEO never ceases to learn. Whether she realizes it or not, performance and tenure may well depend on a strong commitment to *continuing self-education*. The reasons are clear: (a) The CEO's duty to instruct and teach other key members of the staff; (b) the CEO's duty to remain abreast of

---

[1] Used with permission of Heidrick and Struggles, Inc., Chicago, Illinois.

Epilogue

economic developments; (c) the CEO's duty to remain on the leading edge of technological development affecting the business; and (d) the CEO's duty to enhance competitive effectiveness.

Much, much spare time is required for proper study, and the result usually breeds fatigue which, in turn, can raise the stress level discussed in Chapter 10. But adult education can also bring tremendous inner rewards completely apart from the duties of a business executive. As this is written, my thoughts turn to those rare adults, who return to college (in some cases, after more than ten years off campus—including my daughter, Margo) to earn an advanced degree. These role models demonstrate beautifully the clear way in which each one of us can experience rewarding growth—mentally and in every other way—through the discipline of study.

TRADE-OFF NUMBER THREE—CRITICISM

Few things can be more debilitating than unjust criticism—the proverbial "bum wrap." Regrettably it goes with the CEO's territory.

Who among us is immune to the stress caused by criticism? Yet criticism is inevitable for the CEO. *Thicken your skin.* Here's what football great Herschell Walker says about it: "Criticism used to bother me a lot. But now—in my walk through life—I can't really be bothered when I know I've done my best. The critics should always be expected to be there."

Deserved criticism is bad enough, and there is certainly plenty of that with the top job. But everything from your compensation to your perceived hours (what do they know?), your firm decisions (no matter how agonizing), and dozens of other misunderstood aspects of your management style will be targets of criticism. It is often fashionable to "put down" the boss. In some organizations he is feared and even hated at times.

Criticism can also be contagious. When you "catch hell," you tend to want to pass it on. Think it over first and—by all means—never criticize another in the presence of co-workers. Sounds elementary, but it happens almost daily in some of the nation's otherwise best-managed companies. Obviously it will also be to your best interest, when you do find fault privately, to try very hard to acknowledge something done well.

Sometimes it is actually possible to find something so amusing about your undeserved critic or what she has said that you can actually get a lift from it, or possibly even quote it back to others later in a good-natured demonstration of your own broad-gauged tolerance. It works.

Here is an example I have cited many times to make the point. I had been at Texas National, Houston's fourth largest bank, less than 30 days. I knew that my coming in so young at such a high level had caused quite a stir, but the reception up to that time had been quite genuine I thought. One day at noon, however, I stopped at one of the stand-up customer counters in the lobby to cash a check and heard two old nesters talking.

The first was saying, "Have you met the new feller in the bank?"

"Naw, and I'm not sure I want to," said the second.

"Why not?"

"Well, I understand he's a Damn Yankee from Tulsa!"

TRADE-OFF NUMBER FOUR—THE ECONOMY

Whatever business you're in, its own individual market and economic environment will inevitably have its UPS and DOWNS. They will occur completely apart from any effort on your part to prevent or anticipate them. Yet one of your greatest temptations will be to overreact to each extreme. On the upside, you're naturally not as cautious. On the downside, overanxiety can inhibit productive decision making.

Two corollary lessons learned over time—as they say, *the hard way*—are also worth recording here:

1. Markets move in both directions.
2. Avoid excess of all kinds.

The experienced executive recognizes immediately those forces at work in the economy that are beyond his influence or control, that is, the kind CHAPTER 7 was about. His or her talents can then be deployed in ways that are much more likely to yield positive results. This, in fact, is precisely what some are endeavoring to do in those states most affected by the nearly 70 percent decline in energy prices. But it is a remarkable land, and our people

Epilogue

are endowed with a uniquely tough heritage made even stronger by periodic victories over adversity. As a result, the energy slump one day will become but another historic milestone.

"Every bump's a boost" is not a bad philosophy for a CEO whose business plan is subject to economic tides—and they all are.

TRADE-OFF NUMBER FIVE—PATIENCE

Even though the chief executive has the power to decree change within his organization, she is acutely aware of the folly of doing so until there is a constituency formed to insure its success. But it is tough to "trade-off" the clear conviction that a change is needed for days and days of patience until everyone else "sees the light."

People, most of them, are conservative creatures. They get used to things the way they are and resist change almost instinctively. *Sudden change can also create resentment.* If you must try something new, do not rush it. Many good ideas have failed primarily because they were put into effect too rapidly. Give your associates time to adjust their thinking, work out their objectives, and reward your patience.

The best prescription the author has yet found for patience is a constant reminder—however complex the problem—to *start everyday fresh.*

TRADE-OFF NUMBER SIX—MAVERICKS

One lesson I learned very well during my 26 years in command was *never terminate your mavericks—just be prepared to be a little uncomfortable once in a while.* My former associate, vice-chairman Earl Sneed (1914–1979), and I used to console ourselves with this pearl on regular occasions. One of our officers would speak out on some controversial public issue—or support some "extreme" candidate—and our mail would soon literally choke us. But eventually Earl and I began to realize that each of us was also a maverick!

The standard paragraph in my letters to disgruntled customers read, *"In brief, Mr. (or Ms.) _____ , we have learned over the years that the overwhelming majority of our customers prefer to patronize a financial institution where the management makes no effort to tell its officers how to think."* I truly enjoyed signing those letters. I'm certain we lost some business, but the intense loyalty gained from the maverick officer and his or her many followers was far more significant to earning power over time.

And that's my final point about mavericks. The best way to gain loyalty is by giving it when deserved. In my 40 business years I found *no greater reward* than people on my team who were not just going through the motions of making a buck, but genuinely enjoyed their role and were completely loyal to the institution.

TRADE-OFF NUMBER SEVEN—WEALTH

A chief executive is fortunate indeed if his years in office were unaffected by what J.P. Morgan dubbed *"the tyranny of wealth."* His full statement was, "Of all the forms of tyranny the least attractive and the most vulgar is the tyranny of mere wealth, the tyranny of plutocracy."[2]

The misuse of wealth is fairly well guarded against in most sets of corporate bylaws. A strong board committee structure is another preventive measure. Nevertheless the CEO should be aware of the risk as another *occupational hazard* of the career he has chosen.

None of this is to suggest that the officers of a corporation should expect to be able to ignore a controlling ownership—be it "mathematical control" (51 percent ownership) or "effective control" (sometimes much less than a majority). However, one of the trade-offs that comes with being "the boss" is the chance of having one or more "tyrannical bosses" among the owners. Of course, the CEO also may be fortunate enough (as in my own case) to work for many, many years with what I would describe as *enlightened wealth*. Nothing can be more supportive than that—or beneficial to the business.

SO MUCH FOR SOME OF THE PREDOMINANT *TRADE-OFFS* AN ASPIRING CHIEF EXECUTIVE SHOULD EXPECT TO ENCOUNTER.

Little wonder that some of the least happy people I know are CEOs. ARE YOU STILL INTERESTED? NOBODY SAID IT WOULD BE EASY. And this will be so even after you're well on your way. It was the very successful football coach Lou Holtz of

---

[2] J. P. Morgan, "Thoughts on the Business of Life," *Forbes* (October 26, 1987), p. 408.

Epilogue

Notre Dame who said, "I sleep like a baby. . . . I wake up in the middle of the night crying."[3]

Finally, in addition to the ELEVEN BASIC KINDS OF UNDERSTANDING set forth among these pages, a winning chief executive must also either possess or develop the *drive* to get there, the *determination* to stay there, the *judgment* to excel, and the *endurance* to enjoy. And then there's *honesty*. Samuel Goldwyn once said: "The most important thing about acting is *honesty*— once you've learned to fake that, you're in." But a leader never fakes anything. She needs to act like the pro she aspires to be *at all times*.

WHAT KIND OF BOSS WILL YOU BE? *Only you* can respond to that. Meanwhile, be assured that how well you have committed this philosophical little book to memory will not have much effect, for philosophy is only common sense in dress clothes. NO, YOUR OWN COMMON SENSE AND THE LEVEL OF YOUR DESIRE WILL GOVERN.

Isn't it great that every American still has the opportunity to become a CEO? I suppose that's just one of the risks Americans have to take.

Respectfully,
THE AUTHOR

---

[3] CBS-TV Network interview, inter-collegiate football game, Fall 1987.

INDEX

Abernathy, Jack, 73
Accountability, 73
Adams, Dr. Arthur, 88–89
Ailes, Roger, 106–7
Albers School of Business (Seattle University), 14
Alternative leadership styles, 39–40
AMIABLES, 3, 6–7
   backup system, 4, 6–7
   versatility, 8
ANALYSTS, 3, 7
   backup system, 4, 7
   versatility, 9
Annual Career Development and Goal Setting Inventory form, 49
Annual report, 81
Assertive people-oriented types, *See* EXPRESSIVES
Assertive task-oriented types, *See* DRIVERS
Attitude, stress reduction and, 124–25
Austin, Nancy, 36

Backup systems, 4, 127
   resisting, 6–7
Balance, stress reduction and, 125
Balanced vision, failure to develop, 146–47
Bennis, Warren, 36
Berra, Yogi, 60, 75
Board/shareholder relationships, 71–82

board candidacy, criteria for, 80
brevity versus substance, 77–78
"buildup," 75–76
communications, 71–72
ownership myopia, 79–80
shareholder inquiries, 81
ten commandments of communications priorities, 72–75
Bombeck, Erma, 43
Booz-Allen & Hamilton, 65–66
Broader obligations:
   CEOs, 97–110
      alleged gap between business and humanities, 101–2
      customer's bill of rights, 109–10
      definition of term, 97
      ethical dimension, 108–9
      extracurricular activities, 98
      gut decision, 98–99
      heard word, 107
      sociological dimension, 99–100
      spoken word, 105–7
      written word, 102–4
"Buildup," 75–76
Bulwer, Edward George, 1
Burns, James McGregor, 36–37
Bush, George, 98–99
Business purpose, 56
Business Without Economists (Hudson), 83–84
Butterfield, William H., 102–3, 107

Index

CEOs:
  board/shareholder relationships, 71–82
  broader obligations, 97–110
  earning power, 55–70
  leadership, 33–42
  management styles, 13–32
  mistakes (DON'Ts), 21–22
  motivation, 43–54
  self-knowledge, 1–11
  stress, 121–35
  succession, 111–20
  trends/cycle, 83–96
Churchill, Winston, 31, 76
Clawson, James, 23
CNG fuels, secular trends, 87
COACHING style of leadership, 40
Commerciality, 67–68
Commitment, 30–32, 72
Communications, 71–72, 76–79, 81
  ten commandments of communications, 72–75
Community affairs, involvement in, 98
Competition, failure to monitor, 142
Conrad, Joseph, 5
Consensus decision making, 15
Counselor selling, 58
Cover-ups, 73
Credibility, 81
Cribben, James J., 39, 44–45
Crisis management, 19–20
Customer's bill of rights, 109–10
Customer wants/needs, 56–57
Cycles:
  failure to recognize, 141
  length of, 87–89

Dahl, Arlene, 128–29
Danforth, Louis F., 34
Decision diagonal, 15
DELEGATING style of leadership, 40
DIRECTING style of leadership, 40
Disclosure, 73–74
Dividend reinvestment, 81
Drive, 44
DRIVERS, 2, 7
  backup system, 4
    resisting, 7
  versatility, 9
Drucker, Peter Ferdinand, 16–17, 82
Durland, Jack, 40

Earning power, 55–70
  commerciality, 67–68
  goal setting, 60–61
  inward marketing, 69–70
  through organizationwide marketing culture, 55–56
  relationship between problem solving and, 58–59
  research, 59–60
  windfall earnings, 61
Economic research, 17
Edison, Thomas A., 153
Einstein, Albert, 47
Elliott, Dr. William M., Jr., 11
Employee Stock purchase plans, 81
Empowering, 47–51
  declare individuals' importance, 47–48
  demonstrate by example, 50
  explain how action precedes motivation, 50
  make it easy to try, 48
  make it worthwhile to try, 48
  serendipity effect of, 51
ENABLING style of leadership, 40
Entrepreneurship, 37
Ethical dimension, 108–9
  failure to observe, 148–49
Executive committee, 73
Exercise, stress reduction and, 129–30
Expense control, 66
Experts, 4–5
Exploratory technique, of discovering needs, 64
EXPRESSIVES, 3, 8
  backup system, 4
    resisting, 8
  versatility, 9
Extracurricular activities, 98

Failure, 137–54
  to develop balanced vision, 146–47
  to distinguish between tangible products and intangible services, 142–43
  to harness vision, 147–48
  to keep abreast of technology, 141–42
  learning from, 153–54
  to maintain strong organizational structure, 143–44
  to make management/leadership distinction, 149–50
  to monitor competition, 142
  to observe ethical dimension, 148–49
  organization, 152
  to perceive the secular trend, 140–41
  poor personnel selection, 151
  procrastination, 151–52
  to recognize the cyclical trend, 141
  to reject greed, 144–45
  to respect debt, 145–46
  to respect seasonal trends, 141
  to substitute participative management for top-down decision making, 144

Index

to understand definition of success, 150–51
Fears:
of bad morale, 25
banishment of, 47
of displeasing superiors, 44
of embarrassment among peers, 44
Feedback, from subordinate appraisals, 27
Financial reporting, 73
Finn, David, 38
"Forget Ethics—and Succeed?" (Modic), 108
Fuller, R. Buckminster, 86

Gardner, John W., 124
Geneen, Harold, 33, 38–39
Germain, Walter, 138
Goal setting, 19, 60–61, 139
Gordy, Berry, 150–51
Gorges, Denis, 134
Growth-sharing, 129

Hall, John R., 20
Harrison, Richard D., 1–2
Hart, Dr. Hornell, 131
Hay Management Associates, 45–46, 53
Head hunters, CEO succession and, 115–16
Heard word, 107
High technology, 68–69
failure to keep abreast of, 141–42
Hopper, Rear Admiral Grace, 54
House organ articles, 48
Hudson, William J., 83
Humility, 75
Humor, stress reduction and, 125
HYPERACTIVES, 10
Hyperopia, guarding against, 85

Implementation, management planning, 19, 62–64
Incentive compensation, 45, 52
Incentives, 74
Initiative, 30–32
Inner needs, 10
Institutional distinction, 59
Interim objectives, 52–53
Investors, 80–82
Inward marketing, 45–46
earning power and, 69–70
results of empowering others through, 51

JELL management style, 14, 15

Kondratieff, N. D., 88
Kreese, John, 153

Laissez faire, 93–94
Leaders (Bennis/Nanus), 36
Leadership, 33–41
alternative leadership styles, 39–40
definition of, 33–35
versus management, 36–38
ultimate reward, 40–41
what leadership is not, 35–36
Legal exposure, 75
"Letter Analysis Check List" (Butterfield), 103, 104
Lincoln, Abraham, 153
Local media coverage, 48
Losers, masks of, 9–10
Loser's mentality, 138
Loss of employment, stress caused by, 130–31
Luther, John, 53–54

McClelland, David C., 10
McCoy, Chuck, 67
McLean, Barbara, 134
McLean, Larry, 58
Magic Power of Your Mind, The (Germain), 138
Management/leadership distinction, failure to make, 149–50
Management obsolescence, 27–30
Management recommendations, 76
burying, 78
Management styles, 13–32
commitment/initiative, 30–32
crisis management, 19–20
DON'Ts, 21–22, 100, 139
management by "bull session," 15–16
management by objective (MBO), 16–17
master planning model (MPM), 18–29, 139–40
procrastination, 22–23
research, 17–18
subordinate appraisal, 25–27
TELL, SELL, and JELL, 14
Theories X, Y, and Z, 14–16
Management vision, 84–85
Managers, as leaders, 38–39
Marketing, 57–58
Marketing culture:
building of, 58–59
organization-wide, 55–56
Market research, 18
Marvin, Dr. Phillip, 50
Maslow, Abraham H., 63
Maslow Pyramid of Needs, 63
Master planning model (MPM), 18–29, 55, 139–40
Media overkill, 74–75

Mental fatigue, 125–26
Methodology-template, crisis management, 19–20
Miller, Henry, 5
Mintzberg, Henry, 26
Mission statement, redefinition of, 72
Modic, Stanley J., 108
Monitoring, 19, 64–65
  failure to monitor competition, 142
Month-to-month coverage program, 81
Mood meter, 131, 132
  instructions for use of, 133
Motivation, 43–54
  action that precedes, 50
  frailty of others, 43–44
  helpful hints, 47–51
  incentive plan pitfalls, 52–53
  inward marketing, 45–46

Nanus, Burt, 36
Need for achievement, 10
Need for power, 10
Nixon, Richard, 45
Nonassertive people-oriented types, *See* AMIABLES
Nonassertive task-oriented types, *See* ANALYSTS

Obsolete managers, 27–30, 144
Ogilvy, James A., 36
Orben, Robert, 76–77
Organization, failure and, 152
Organizational research, 18
Ownership myopia, 79–80

Participative management (PM), failure to substitute for top-down decision making, 144
Passion for Excellence, A (Peters/Austin), 36
Peale, Norman Vincent, 138
People knowledge, 62
Performance evaluations, 48
Personal esteem, need for, 63–64
Personality grid, 2, 3, 8
  versatility scale, 3, 4
Personnel selection, failure and, 151
Peters, Tom, 36
Pfizer, Beryl, 105–6
Physical comfort, need for, 63
Pickens, T. Boone, 37, 84
Planagement (Randolph), 27–30
Planning, 19, 61–62
Polucci, Jeno, 44
Positive thinking, 138
Power of Positive Thinking, The (Peale), 138

Preemptive rights, 79
Prima donna tendency, 6–8
Procrastination, 22–23, 151–52
Product knowledge, 62
Psychology of Winning (Waitley), 138

Randolph, Robert M., 27–30
Random trends, 90
Reality, stress reduction and, 126–27
Reed, John S., 87
Regulation Q, 93
Release, stress reduction and, 127–29
Research, 17–18, 59–60
  coverage, 81
Respect for debt, 146
Revson, Charles, 57
Rilke, Ranier Maria, 91
Rinfret, Pierre A., 88
Risks:
  leadership, 37–38, 40–41
  risk of failure, 152–53
Rockefeller, John D., 124–25
Rogers, Will, 43
Rosenberg, Merri, 130–31
Ruth, Babe, 153

Schwab, Charles, 91
Search firms, CEO succession and, 115–16
Seasonal trends, 89–90
  failure to respect, 141
Secular trends, 85–87
  failure to perceive, 140–41
  sensing emergence of, 86–87
Security, need for, 63
Self-appraisal exam, 23–25
Self-discipline, 50
Self-knowledge, 1–11
Selflessness, stress reduction and, 129
Selling, versus marketing, 57
SELL management style, 14, 15
Service, retaining customers through, 59
Simplification, stress reduction and, 126
Sinatra, Frank, 152–53
Skills, development of, 62
SKIPPERS, 9
Social acceptance, need for, 63
Sociological dimension, 99–100
Spoken word, 105–7
Stress:
  CEOs, 121–35
    exercises nobody needs, 122
    loss of employment, 130–31
    mood meter, 131
    remedies, 124–30
    remembering your roots, 134

Index

stress levels, 122–24
Synchro-Energizer, 134
Subconscious versatility, 11
Subordinate appraisals:
  of CEOs, 25–27
  feedback from, 27
SUBTLE CYNICS, 9–10
Success, failure to understand true definition of, 150–51
Succession:
  CEO, 111–20
    candidate scorecard, 113
    classic case, 111–14
    clean exit, 117–18
    feelings/relationships, 114–15
    internal versus external successor, 115–16
    outward behavior characteristics, 115
    pitfalls, 116–17
    thinking, 114
    ultimate asset, 118–19
Superior customer service, 65–66
"Supervisor's Prayer" (Luther), 53–54
Supervisory appraisal, of CEOs, 26
Synchro-Energizer, 134

Technological change, 68–69
TELL management style, 14, 15
Texaco, 66–67
Theories X, Y, and Z, 14–16, 39
Trade-offs, 155–61
  criticism, 157–58
  the economy, 158–59
  family, 156
  mavericks, 159–60
  patience, 159
  study, 156–57
  wealth, 160–61
Transactional leadership, 37
Transformative leadership, 37

Trends/cycles, 83–95
  coping with, 91–93
    independence, 92–93
    observation, 91–92
  cycles, length of, 87–89
  laissez faire, 93–94
  negatives, dealing with, 94–95
  random trends, 90
  seasonal trends, 89–90
  secular trends, 85–87
    sensing emergence of, 86–87
Truman, Harry S., 47

ULTRACONSERVERS, 10
Unrealistic expectations, 126–27

Versatility:
individual growth and, 8–9
subconscious versatility, 11
versatility scale, 4
Vision:
  balanced, failure to develop, 146–47
  failure to harness, 147–48
  management, 84–85

Waitley, Denis E., 138
Wheat, Dr. Willis J., 38
"When You Write a Letter . . . Make Every Word Count" (Butterfield), 103
Whittle, Jack, 59
Williams, Tennessee, 153
Wilson, Larry, 2, 58
Wilson Learning Company, 2, 14
Windfall earnings, 61
Worldwide Energy System, A (Fuller), 86
Wright, Don, 152
Wriston, Walter, 68–69, 111
Written word, 102–4

You Are the Message (Ailes), 106–7